A New Guide to Post Keynesian Economics

How do Post Keynesian economists view the rising inequality occurring throughout the world?

What do Post Keynesian economists think about the state and government budget deficits and surpluses?

What is the Post Keynesian approach to macroeconomics?

A sequel to Alfred Eichner's seminal 1978 volume, *A Guide to Post Keynesian Economics*, this edited volume provides a comprehensive introduction to the Post Keynesian position on key issues confronting economists and policy-makers. The *New Guide* reflects the changes in Post Keynesian thought as well as developments that have taken place in the world economy since the 1970s. Covering such areas as methodology, uncertainty and expectations, distribution, pricing, tax incidence, macrodynamics, inflation, labor and unemployment, theory of state, and international finance, this book provides an outstanding introduction for undergraduate and graduate students to the Post Keynesian view on how today's economy works and how to improve economic performance.

- Each chapter is written clearly and will be accessible to both undergraduate and graduate students.
- Mathematical equations and technical material are kept to a bare minimum.
- Each chapter discusses the Post Keynesian view on one particular topic and contrasts that view with the orthodox perspective on that topic.
- All chapters conclude with a discussion of the policy implications of Post Keynesian analysis.

Richard P.F. Holt is Associate Professor of Economics at Southern Oregon University. He also serves as General Editor and Electronic Manager of *Post Keynesian Thought*.

Steven Pressman is Professor of Economics and Finance at Monmouth University. He also serves as North American Editor of the *Review of Political Economy*.

Contemporary political economy series
Edited by Jonathan Michie
Birkbeck College, University of London

This series presents a fresh, broad perspective on the key issues in the modern world economy, drawing in perspectives from management and business, politics and sociology, economic history and law.

Written in a lively and accessible style, it will present focused and comprehensive introductions to key topics, demonstrating the relevance of political economy to major debates in economics and to an understanding of the contemporary world.

Global Instability
The political economy of world economic governance
Edited by Jonathan Michie and John Grieve Smith

Reconstructing Political Economy
The great divide in economic thought
William K. Tabb

The Political Economy of Competitiveness
Employment, public policy and corporate performance
Michael Kitson and Jonathan Michie

Global Economy, Global Justice
Theoretical objections and policy alternatives to neoliberalism
George F. DeMartino

Social Capital Versus Social Theory
Political economy and social science at the turn of the millennium
Ben Fine

A New Guide to Post Keynesian Economics
Edited by Richard P.F. Holt and Steven Pressman

ost

ics

d

DGE
Francis Group

on and New York

First published 2001
by Routledge
11 New Fetter Lane, London EC4P 4EE

Simultaneously published in the USA and Canada
by Routledge
29 West 35th Street, New York, NY 10001

Routledge is an imprint of the Taylor & Francis Group

© 2001 edited by Richard P.F. Holt and Steven Pressman

Typeset in Garamond by
Prepress Projects Ltd, Perth, Scotland
Printed and bound in Malta by
Gutenberg Press

British Library Cataloguing in Publication Data
A catalogue record for this book is available
from the British Library

Library of Congress Cataloging in Publication Data

Holt, Richard P. F., 1953–
    A new guide to post Keynesian economics / Richard P. F. Holt and Steven Pressman
        p. cm – (Contemporary political economy)
    Includes bibliographical references and index.
        1. Keynesian economics. I. Pressman, Steven. II. Title. III.
    Contemporary political economy series
    HB99.7.H65 2001
    330.15′6–dc21   2001020408

    ISBN 0-415-22981-2 – ISBN 0-415-22982-0 (pbk)

For Al Eichner, who conceived the *Guide to Post Keynesian Economics*

Contents

Figures

Contributors

Sheila Dow is Professor of Economics at the University of Stirling, UK. She worked for the Bank of England and the Department of Finance of the Government of Manitoba. She is the author of numerous journal articles and books in methodology, the history of economic thought, monetary theory and regional finance, including *The Methodology of Macroeconomic Thought*.

James K. Galbraith is Professor at the Lyndon B. Johnson School of Public Affairs and the Department of Government at the University of Texas at Austin. He is also director of the University of Texas Inequality Project and Senior Scholar at the Jerome Levy Economics Institute. He frequently contributes to *The American Prospect*, *Challenge*, and the *Texas Observer*, and he is the author of *Balancing Acts: Technology, Finance and the American Future* and *Created Unequal: The Crisis in American Pay*.

Richard P. F. Holt is Associate Professor of Economics at Southern Oregon University. He has published in scholarly journals such as the *Review of Political Economy*, the *Eastern Economic Journal* and the *Journal of Economic History*. He is co-editor of *Economics and its Discontents: Twentieth Century Dissenting Economists* and serves as General Editor and Electronic Manager of *Post Keynesian Thought* (PKT).

John E. King is Reader in Economics at La Trobe University, Australia. His main research interests are the history of economic thought, with special reference to Marxian political economy and post Keynesian theory. He is the author or editor of numerous books, including *A Bibliography of Post Keynesian Economics* and *Conversations with Post Keynesians*.

Anthony J. Laramie is Professor of Economics at Merrimack College, USA. He is the co-author (with Douglas Mair) of numerous papers on Kaleckian public finance, which have been published in such journals as the *Cambridge Journal of Economics* and the *Journal of Post Keynesian Economics*. He is also co-author (with Douglas Mair) of *A Dynamic Theory of Taxation: Integrating Kalecki into Modern Public Finance*.

Marc Lavoie is Professor of Economics at the University of Ottawa, Canada. He is the co-editor or author of five books, and has published over 100 articles, mainly in the fields of monetary economics, growth theory, and sports economics. He has been a Visiting Professor at the Universities of Bordeaux, Nice, Rennes, Dijon, and Grenoble, and at Curtin University.

Douglas Mair is Professor of Economics at Heriot-Watt University, UK. He is the co-author (with Anthony J. Laramie) of numerous papers on Kaleckian public finance in the *Cambridge Journal of Economics,* and the *Journal of Post Keynesian Economics.* He is also co-author (with Anthony J. Laramie) of *A Dynamic Theory of Taxation: Integrating Kalecki into Modern Public Finance.*

Steven Pressman is Professor of Economics and Finance at Monmouth University. He also serves as Associate Editor of the *Eastern Economic Journal,* North American Editor of the *Review of Political Economy,* and Treasurer of the Eastern Economic Association. He has written or edited seven books, including *Fifty Major Economists,* and has published more than sixty articles in books and refereed journals.

J. Barkley Rosser Jr is Professor of Economics and Kirby L. Kramer Jr Professor at James Madison University. He is the author of three books and numerous articles. He is Editor in Chief of the *Journal of Economic Behavior and Organization,* Book Review Editor of *Discrete Dynamics in Nature and Society,* and serves on the Editorial Board of *Nonlinear Dynamics in Psychology and Life Sciences* and the *Journal of Post Keynesian Economics.*

Mark Setterfield is Associate Professor of Economics at Trinity College, Hartford, CT. He is the author of *Rapid Growth and Relative Decline: Modelling Macroeconomic Dynamics with Hysteresis,* the editor of *Growth, Employment and Inflation: Essays in Honour of John Cornwall,* and has published in numerous journals including the *Cambridge Journal of Economics, European Economic Review, Journal of Post Keynesian Economics and The Manchester School.*

John Smithin is Professor of Economics in the Department of Economics and Schulich School of Business, York University, Canada. He is author or co-editor of numerous books including *Controversies in Monetary Economics; Macroeconomic Policy and the Future of Capitalism; Money, Financial Institutions and Macroeconomics;* and *What is Money?*

L. Randall Wray is Professor of Economics and a senior research associate of the Center for Full Employment and Price Stability at the University of Missouri – Kansas City. He is the author of *Money and Credit in Capitalist Economies* and *Understanding Modern Money* and has contributed to numerous professional journals including the *Cambridge Journal of Economics, Journal of Post Keynesian Economics, Journal of Economic Issues,* and *Review of Political Economy.*

Foreword

Joan Robinson wrote the Foreword to the first *Guide to Post-Keynesian Economics* (Eichner, 1978). She concluded that the authors of the various essays, by "throwing off the paralysis of neoclassical equilibrium" were "explaining ... the problems of prices, employment, distribution, growth and stagflation in the actual, historical evolution of an ever changing world." She did not expect definitive answers to be found quickly so "there [was] plenty of work still to do" (Robinson, 1979: xxi). The essays in the present *Guide* are progress reports on the response to her challenge.

But hers was not the only challenge that had to be faced over the intervening years. Those decades saw the rise of monetarism and new classical macroeconomics, both as the dominant approach to theory and as the rationale for policy. While there have been signs recently that New Keynesian theory has been making an effective counterattack, and that the most harsh policies of the 1970s, 1980s, and 1990s are being modified, there is little doubt that we still live in an era that Robinson (1964) herself memorably dubbed (even before it occurred) "Pre-Keynesian theory [and policy] after Keynes." Short-period real business cycle and long-period endogenous growth happenings are overwhelmingly analyzed by using representative agent models, where the representative agent is often a Ramsey maximizer. How Frank Ramsey would have squirmed to have seen his conception so grossly misplaced and misused. Even in its proper setting he was pretty scathing about it. In a letter to Keynes (26 June 1928), which he enclosed with his paper on a mathematical theory of saving for the *Economic Journal*, Ramsey (1928) wrote, "Of course the whole thing is a waste of time." It had distracted him from "a book on logic [because] it [was] much easier to concentrate on than philosophy and the difficulties that arise rather [obsessed him]" (Keynes, 1983: 784).

The overlap between these models and views of the world, and those which characterize the Post Keynesian approach, is little to non-existent. As Chari (1998) pointed out in his laudatory evaluation of the contributions of Robert Lucas, macroeconomics has never been the same since Lucas came upon the scene. (Whether it has improved or advanced is another matter.) I spoke recently to the World Conference of Social Economists who were meeting in Cambridge on what Marx and Keynes would have made of the last thirty years or so of economic events and economic theory. I suggested that they would have had little trouble in identifying why things had happened as they did, though their reactions would have differed markedly. Keynes would have sat down to try once again to save capitalism from itself. Marx may have rubbed his hands and hoped that this time the basic contradictions he had identified, not least the instability and crises associated with financial capital on the one hand and industrial and commercial capital on the other no longer moving in tandem, would bring down the whole system. (Better late than never!)

There has been a sea of change in institutions and attitudes and great technical advances, especially in information technology, which has drastically reduced the historical length of the short run in key markets, many of which have been deregulated. Political norms and constraints have also changed greatly so that policies proposed now have to operate in much changed climates of possibility and acceptance. The economics profession itself, often because of its own misdeeds and immodesty, is regarded in many quarters with ridicule and often with hostility, dislike, and contempt.

Such a configuration of events is peculiarly opportune for the messages that the authors of the essays in this volume are bringing, especially for students. They report a body of work that has as its starting point the world as it is. Theory on each issue is built up from detailed observations of both individual and collective aggregate behavior suitably simplified to make them intelligible and manageable within models of the interrelationships between them. The understandings so gained of the processes at work are the necessary prerequisites for thinking about appropriate and relevant policies with which to tackle the malfunctionings revealed and explained. Post Keynesian economics is first and foremost fruit-bearing in the Pigovian sense. Any light-bearing involved is always a means, never an end in itself.

The twelve chapters in the volume cover a wide range of absorbing issues. The editors tell us what the subject matter is in the opening chapter and where we are heading in the closing chapter. They are enthusiastic and knowledgeable guides, warm-hearted and clear-headed, with fire in their bellies, ideal persons to guide and inspire. Sheila Dow has made seminal contributions to our understanding of Post Keynesian methodology. She has written a lucid account of origins and developments, drawing attention to disagreements as well as agreements – a good thing too. In any healthy development of an approach, useful argument is much to be preferred to slavish discipleship or censorious hegemony.

A feature of Post Keynesian economics has always been dissatisfaction with conventional theories of prices, combined with attempts (both theoretical and empirical) to provide more satisfactory and realistic alternatives. Partly this has been done in order to chart the richness of different behaviors between different industries, market structures, and activities of the economy; partly the objective has been to provide a simple but coherent account of price formation to be fitted into models of the macroeconomic processes at work in advanced capitalist economies. Marc Lavoie provides a comprehensive account of these developments from the beginnings to the present time.

The distribution of income has also been a central focus of Post Keynesian economics. This reflects its links back to the classical political economists and Marx, and also the concern of its practitioners for the lot of the least fortunate in society. James Galbraith has done more than most to enhance our understanding of these complex processes. He contributes a progress report on the contributions generally and on some of his latest contributions in particular.

Anthony Laramie and Douglas Mair have made sustained and sterling contributions to the important, complicated topic of the theory of the incidence of different taxes when the economy is modeled in a Kaleckian framework. They report the findings of this literature and what the future agenda contains.

In Chapter 6 Barkley Rosser Jr. rightly emphasizes the deep problems associated with the inescapable fact that key economic decisions must always be made in an environment of uncertainty. Because the theory of rational expectations assumes that the world may be viewed "as if" perfect competition and perfect foresight reigned, and that a coherent body of theory worked out on the basis of this assumption is directly applicable to that world, Post Keynesians must reject any body of work that incorporates rational expectations. This includes New Keynesian economics. At a theoretical level we still have much to do in order to understand how individual decision makers and the system itself respond to the uncertain environment. The policy agenda is to change institutions and policies in an attempt to minimize the impact of uncertainty on individual and systemic behavior. This is more easily said than done as anyone who has tried to construct appropriate policies knows only too well, but it has to be faced and worked at. Rosser tells us how we are doing and what else (a lot) has to be done.

John King follows on from Eileen Appelbaum's (1979) excellent chapter on the labor market in the first *Guide*, with an essay on labor and unemployment. He brings to it his encyclopedic knowledge of the history of our subject and his own expertise in labor economics. Always clear and skeptical, he is the very model of a sympathetic yet critical reporter.

The last four chapters – Randall Wray on money and inflation, Mark Setterfield on macrodynamics, Steve Pressman on the role of the state, and John Smithin on international monetary arrangements – are important complements to one another. The authors have made original contributions to their respective topics and they bring their collective wisdom to bear in order to provide their progress reports. In a very changed political climate, rethinking on the role of the state, both as it is now and realistically what Post Keynesians would like it to be, is a top priority. To underpin this we need (and we get here) fundamental rethinking about inflationary processes and the role of money, the nature of the macrodynamic processes at work in modern economies (Mark Setterfield and his mentor, John Cornwall, lead the way here) and how we may design international institutions and domestic policies to tackle the malfunctionings of the international system which Keynes and others identified at Bretton Woods and tried (but ultimately failed) to offset through the creation of the IMF and the World Bank.

I hope Joan Robinson would have been delighted with the extensions and advances that have been made by young Post Keynesian scholars since she wrote her Foreword. She herself was very pessimistic in her last years, but there is clear evidence in these pages that people have responded to her more optimistic phase and kept her flame alight. It is profoundly to be hoped that those students who are introduced to these essays by their teachers (or, even more so, through their own initiative) respond as enthusiastically and intelligently as have the authors of the essays and the authors in the literature they have reported so ably.

Geoff C. Harcourt
Jesus College
Cambridge

References

Appelbaum, E. (1979) "The Labor Market," in A.S. Eichner (ed.) *A Guide to Post Keynesian Economics*, Armonk, NY: M.E. Sharpe, pp. 100–19.

Chari, V. (1998) "Nobel Laureate Robert E. Lucas, Jr: Architect of Modern Macroeconomics," *Journal of Economic Perspectives*, 12: 171–86.

Eichner, A.S. (ed.) (1978) *A Guide to Post Keynesian Economics*, Armonk, NY: M.E. Sharpe.

Keynes, J.M. (1983) *The Collected Writings of John Maynard Keynes*, vol. XII, London: Macmillan.

Ramsey, F.P. (1928) "A Mathematical Theory of Saving," *Economic Journal*, 38: 543–59.

Robinson, J. (1964) "Pre-Keynesian Theory after Keynes," *Australian Economic Papers*, 3: 25–35.

Robinson, Joan (1979) "Foreword," in A.S. Eichner (ed.) *A Guide to Post Keynesian Economics*, Armonk, NY: M.E. Sharpe, pp. xi–xxi.

1 What is Post Keynesian economics?

Richard P.F. Holt and Steven Pressman

Introduction

A Guide to Post Keynesian Economics was published in 1978. This slim volume, edited by Alfred Eichner, provided a non-technical introduction to Post Keynesian thought. It contained essays from some major Post Keynesian figures on key economic issues of the day. Many undergraduate and graduate students received their primary exposure to Post Keynesian economics from this book; and many of our colleagues have told us that they first learned about Post Keynesian economics from reading it.

While the Eichner volume was a useful resource in the late 1970s and early 1980s, it is less useful today because so much has changed over the last two decades.

First, there have been important changes in the world economy. The collapse of the former Soviet Union and the fall of Communist governments in Eastern Europe led to a profound change in the world economic order. Victorious in its war with Communism, Capitalism asserted its virtues; as a result, in country after country government regulations were reduced in the 1990s and the market was given greater sway over economic life. In addition, the last two decades have witnessed rapid advances in transportation and information technologies. These changes have allowed dramatic increases in international trade and capital mobility, as world markets have opened up. They have also resulted in two major international financial system crises. The first occurred in the 1980s, when many developing countries, particularly in Latin America, came close to defaulting on their international loans. The second crisis occurred in the 1990s, when many Asian countries experienced declining currencies and stock markets after banks and firms could not service their debts. Both of these crises exposed the fragility of our international financial system in a world of great capital mobility.

The past twenty-five years have also seen major changes within the economic profession. This is especially true of macroeconomics. During the 1970s, the central issue in macroeconomics was the controversy between Keynesians and Monetarists. At the beginning of the twenty-first century macroeconomic analysis begins with the contributions of the new classical economists, who believe that markets are stable and promote long-term growth, and that microeconomic principles must explain macroeconomic outcomes. This has had some important consequences. With the development of rational expectations many economists now hold that economic policies have little or no affect on real output, thus leaving *laissez-faire* as the policy prescription of choice. They also hold that capitalist economies, driven by the rationality of their main economic actors, will tend to attain full employment of all existing resources, including labor.

Finally, substantive changes have taken place within the Post Keynesian paradigm itself. Many key ideas have been both expanded and developed. Post Keynesians have analyzed the pricing decision of firms more carefully; and they have developed their analyses of unemployment, inflation, income distribution and uncertainty. Many gaps in Post Keynesian thought have been filled also. Post Keynesians have begun to discuss methodological issues and they have been forced to think more about the role of the state in economic affairs. There has also been a major rift between the Sraffians and the Post Keynesians, and Post Keynesians have begun to discuss the coherence or consistency of their economic vision (Dunn, 2000).

Because of these many changes, there is a need for a new introduction to the ideas of the Post Keynesians (for recent scholarly accounts of Post Keynesian economics see Lavoie, 1992; Arestis, 1992, 1996; Davidson, 1994). That is what this volume is all about. It is designed to provide a contemporary and up-to-date introduction to Post Keynesian thought for students and for our professional colleagues.

This introduction traces the historical development of Post Keynesian economics. It begins, logically, with Keynes and his contemporaries and colleagues, the first generation of Post Keynesians. Then it summarizes the contributions of the second generation of Post Keynesians. In most cases, these economists were influenced by reading the *General Theory*, and they studied under, or were influenced by, some first-generation Post Keynesians. Finally, we conclude with a summary of the articles contained in this volume. These articles have been written by third-generation Post Keynesians. In many cases, the authors of this volume were students or protégés of the second generation of Post Keynesians who contributed to the first *Guide*.

The development of Post Keynesian thinking

Post Keynesian economics starts with the work of Keynes, especially his *General Theory of Employment, Interest and Money* (Keynes [1936] 1964). This work threw down the gauntlet and challenged established economic thinking in numerous ways.

Much ink has been spilt about what Keynes meant in the *General Theory* and what his challenge to orthodoxy actually was. Although these questions remain a matter of debate, it is generally accepted that the *General Theory* began the serious study of macroeconomics. It explained the factors that determined levels of output and employment for a particular economy; it explained how and why economies could experience low levels of output and high levels of unemployment for long periods of time; and it provided a framework for formulating economic policies that would lead to improved economic performance.

For Keynes, as well as for Post Keynesians, it is demand that drives the overall economy. Total or aggregate demand is affected by a number of important variables – income distribution, uncertainty, the psychological habits of consumers, the "animal spirits" of entrepreneurs, and government policies. Total demand, in turn, has important economic consequences. It determines the levels of unemployment and inflation, it affects the distribution of income, and it determines the extent of government budget deficits and national trade deficits.

Another important influence on Post Keynesian thought was the work of Polish economist Michal Kalecki (see Sawyer, 1985, 1998). Independently of Keynes, Kalecki developed a theory of the business cycle emphasizing the importance of demand. But unlike Keynes, Kalecki assumed differing degrees of competition among firms; and he cast his analysis of the business cycle in terms of different classes and different economic sectors. Expectations drove investment spending, which made the economy run. But changing expectations generated potential instabilities. Unlike neoclassical theory, but like classical economic theory, for Kalecki the degree of monopoly determines how high firms can set prices, and thus the distribution of income between wages and profits. Income distribution, in turn, affects demand.

Following Keynes and Kalecki came the work of Joan Robinson and Nicholas Kaldor. Robinson (1980, vol. 5: 48–58) emphasized the role of history as opposed to equilibrium in doing economic analysis. For Robinson, the notion of stability inherent in equilibrium analysis was inappropriate for a discipline like economics which deals with growing and changing economies. She also stressed that the real world was not like the world of perfect competition portrayed in economic textbooks. Rather, according to Robinson (1933), most industries comprised large firms wielding extensive market power. This dovetailed with Kalecki's analysis of pricing and income distribution. Robinson (1980, vol. 2: 114–31) also began the so-called Cambridge Controversy with her critique of the marginalist theory of distribution (see Harcourt, 1972). This opened the way for a Post Keynesian, class-based analysis of income distribution.

Kaldor came to Cambridge from the London School of Economics, and although he was never entirely comfortable with the economics developed at Cambridge, he did contribute several important ideas to the Post Keynesian corpus. Kaldor was interested in growth and in economic policy. He used sectoral analysis (Kaldor, 1967), an idea going back to the classical thinkers, to argue that economic growth required a dynamic manufacturing sector. Kaldor (1982) was also instrumental in fighting monetarism and developing the Post Keynesian view that money was endogenous – the supply of money was determined by the need of firms for loans to expand their operations and by the need of banks to earn profits from making loans, rather than by the monetary policies of the central bank (for more on Kaldor, see Pressman, 1998).

Also in Cambridge during this time was Piero Sraffa. Although he wrote very little, his influence was profound. In the 1920s he published a path-breaking article that attacked supply and demand analysis by pointing out logical flaws in the Marshallian theory of the firm (Sraffa, 1926). Sraffa (1960) then sought to bring back to life the Ricardian theory of value. His book *Production of Commodities By Means of Commodities* shows that the neoclassical theory of value is circular and needs to be replaced by the more logically consistent theory of value whose roots can be found in Ricardo. Sraffa's work led to a "Classical Revival" in the 1960s and 1970s. Sraffa, along with Robinson and Kaldor, inspired a new generation of economists at Cambridge during the 1950s and 1960s, including Tom Asimakopulos, Piero Garegnani, Luigi Pasinetti, and Geoff Harcourt.

Asimakopulos (1971; 1991), in many ways, was the gadfly among the Post Keynesians. He insisted that Keynes's ideas be clarified and that Kalecki's insights be seriously considered. He developed a critique of Keynes's theory of investment in the *General Theory* because it ignored the role of historical time and uncertainty. He then sought to develop a more satisfactory Post Keynesian theory of investment. Garegnani (1960), with Sraffa, developed a critique of the marginalist theory of distribution, thereby opening the door for alternative distribution theories. A leading member of this generation is Lugi L. Pasinetti, who extended Sraffa's work with a rigorous mathematical formulation of Ricardo's theory of value and distribution (Pasinetti, 1960). Building on the work of Kaldor, Pasinetti (1962) also helped develop a non-marginalist theory of distribution, which showed that the rate of profit in an economy is dependent on the growth rate and the propensity of capitalists to save.

Finally, Harcourt (1972) is probably best known for his famous review of the Cambridge Capital Controversy. With his clear and humorous writing style, Harcourt was able to take this obscure debate and make it understandable to many economists and to show the theoretical importance of the debate. During the 1960s and 1970s Harcourt wrote a series of important and influential papers on the theory of price setting and markups, exemplified by his two-sector model (1965) and his article with Peter Kenyon in which they explain the size of markups by firms in terms of the financial requirements of firms (1976).

John Kenneth Galbraith helped build the bridge between the European and American Post Keynesians. Galbraith (1967; along with Alfred Eichner, 1976) developed the insights of Robinson on imperfect competition. He noted that "the market," which forms the basis for most economic analysis, was replaced by "the planning" done by large oligopolies, which produce most of the goods we purchase. This market power allows firms to control wages and prices. One consequence of this analysis is that an incomes policy, or some form of wage and price control by the government, is a better way to control inflation than macroeconomic policies that throw people out of work (Galbraith, 1952; Weintraub and Wallich, 1978).

The second generation of American Post Keynesians begins with Sidney Weintraub and Paul Davidson. In 1978, with financial support from Galbraith, Weintraub and Davidson began editing the *Journal of Post Keynesian Economics*. It has since served as an important research outlet and communication vehicle for Post Keynesians.

Weintraub became interested in Keynes after reading the *General Theory*. He soon recognized that traditional Keynesian economics, as represented by the 45° line model and the IS–LM model, ignored supply-side factors. It also ignored prices and price changes, yet talked about such things as "inflation" and "inflationary gaps" (Weintraub, 1961). Weintraub argued that these models should be abandoned in favor of an aggregate supply–aggregate demand model, which would better represent the insights of Keynes. Weintraub (1958) went on to develop such a model. He then extended this model in order to analyze important macroeconomic issues like growth and distribution (Weintraub, 1966).

Davidson, a student of Weintraub's at the University of Pennsylvania, went to Cambridge to work on *Money and the Real World* (Davidson, 1972). This book became a seminal work in the interpretation of Keynes and the development of a Post Keynesian view of money (Holt *et al.*, 1998). Davidson pointed out that production takes time. Money must be borrowed now and repaid later. As a result, all economies exist in real, historical time. The present state of the economy is in large part determined by the state of the economy in the recent past. And to understand where real economies are heading, we need to know the recent past as well as any recent changes in expectations, policies, or other important factors affecting the economy.

Davidson (1972; 1982) argued that it is the nature of money that causes unemployment according to Keynes. Money is different from other goods in one fundamental respect. If people wish to hold money and do not buy goods, business sales fall and workers get laid off. Davidson has also argued that it is uncertainty that makes the world unpredictable, and that makes people want to hold money.

Other important figures helped to develop the economic vision of Keynes. Hyman Minsky (1982) added an analysis of the financial system that helped to explain market crashes and business cycles. The Great Depression and the stock market crash of 1929 intrigued Minsky. He spent many years trying to understand what caused the great speculative bubble of the 1920s, believing this to be the key cause of the 1929 crash, the Great Depression, and the immense human suffering that resulted. His studies focused on debt and debt ratios during economic expansions. Minsky explained how optimism leads to greater debt and more risky investments, thus setting the stage for a sharp economic decline. He also explained how and why human psychological dispositions lead to cycles of optimism and debt, and how this creates instability in the financial system. Financial instability, in turn, leads to instability in the level of investment and business fluctuations.

As noted earlier, traditional economic theory views money as primarily exogenous. The stock of money in the economy is taken as determined primarily by decisions made by the central bank. When central banks want to expand economic activity, they use their monetary policy tools, thereby giving banks more reserves that can be lent out. The lending activity then creates money. Based on this reasoning, the money supply is usually drawn as a vertical line – fixed and controlled by central bank policy.

Basil Moore (1988) picked up on the work of Kaldor and developed the Post Keynesian doctrine that the money supply should be drawn as a horizontal line because central banks control interest rates and interest rates alone. Given the rate of interest, the money supply is determined by the demand for loans. Because banks make money by lending, they will tend to lend out as much as they can; their only constraint is the demand for loans. An important implication of this analysis is that there are limits to monetary policy, for central banks cannot control the demand for loans. As a result, fiscal policy should be more effective than monetary policy in dealing with macroeconomic issues such as growth, unemployment, and inflation.

All of this was pretty much the conventional wisdom when the first *Guide* was published. Some of these ideas needed further development, which has taken place over the past twenty years or so. In addition, as we saw earlier, new issues and problems arose in the latter half of the 1970s, in the 1980s, and in the 1990s. Third-generation Post Keynesian economists, who authored the essays in the volume, have responded to these challenges.

The new Post Keynesian guide

In the 1970s, economists did not concern themselves very much with methodological issues. They tended to follow the methodology of Milton Friedman (1953), who stressed instrumentalism – good theories are theories that work. In addition, according to the standard methodological precepts, all economics must be based on the assumption of individual rationality.

Post Keynesians adopt a rather different set of methodological principles. They pride themselves on being realistic rather than abstract, and they seek to understand the problems facing real world economies. People actually behave by following rules, developing habits, seeing what others do, etc. And business executives follow what Keynes called their "animal spirits" rather than rationality. This involves using intuition and educated guesses to decide whether to expand, where to expand, and how to expand the firm. Because problems differ and individual motivations differ, Post Keynesians use different approaches and techniques, depending on the situation. This open and pluralistic approach is discussed in greater detail by Sheila Dow in Chapter 2.

Given their emphasis on looking at real economies and how they work, Post Keynesians reject the neoclassical view that most industries comprise a large number of highly competitive firms that exercise no control over prices and are subject to the whims and changing tastes of consumers. Since large firms are price makers rather than price takers, some theory is needed to explain how firms actually go about setting prices. Post Keynesians emphasize markup or cost-plus pricing – firms add a percentage to their cost of producing goods. The markup is determined in part by custom and in part by the needs of each firm for funds that will enable it to invest and expand. In Chapter 3, Marc Lavoie explains some of the different Post Keynesian views on how firms actually set prices, and contrasts the Post Keynesian vision with the neoclassical vision. The key difference, and one of the salient defining characteristics of the Post Keynesian paradigm, is that for Post Keynesians prices reflect the cost of production rather than scarcity.

For neoclassical economics, income distribution is a microeconomic phenomenon and depends on individual marginal productivities. Despite the capital critique (Harcourt, 1972), which pointed out a serious logical flaw in this analysis, neoclassical economics persists in using this approach to study questions regarding income distribution. In Chapter 4 of this volume, James Galbraith presents a different way to understand income distribution. Rather than focusing on microeconomic factors, he examines the macroeconomic causes of income inequality. And rather than focusing on supply-side factors (like human capital accumulation) that affect income distribution, he focuses on demand-side factors. In particular, Galbraith shows that rapid economic growth tends to make the personal distribution of income more equal, and that slow growth generally causes inequality to rise.

In Chapter 5, Tony Laramie and Douglas Mair apply Post Keynesian principles to the issue of taxation. Neoclassical economists look at just the microeconomic effects of taxes. Their concern is how tax rates affect individual behavior. Higher taxes are a disincentive for certain types of behavior, and the higher the tax rate the more an activity gets discouraged. Post Keynesians put more emphasis on the distributional consequences of tax policy and the effects of changes in distribution on spending and macroeconomic outcomes. In brief, Laramie and Mair show how the income effects of taxation exceed the substitution effects and what the policy implications are of this perspective.

Chapter 6 begins the focus on more macroeconomic concerns. J. Barkley Rosser Jr points out in this chapter that fundamental to Post Keynesian macroeconomic analysis is the idea that the future is unknowable or uncertain. As a result, economic actors cannot make probability judgments about profits expected in the future. Profit expectations, to the extent that they affect investment decisions, thus depend on things like habits and conventions, which can easily shift. When they do shift, economies are affected. And when profit expectations are poor, economies will experience severe unemployment, for there will be little investment and little spending. Rosser also points out that Keynesian uncertainty undermines the rational expectations hypothesis that has been used to argue against active macroeconomic policy

In Chapter 7, John King explains in greater detail the Post Keynesian view of unemployment and the workings of labor markets. Again, for Post Keynesians, the focus of analysis is at the macroeconomic level rather than the microeconomic level. Unemployment, according to Post Keynesians, results from insufficient aggregate demand rather than from excessively high wage rates in the labor market. Similarly, wage differentials are looked at as the consequence of discrimination by oligopolistic employers (a macroeconomic issue) rather than inadequacies of members of some group (a microeconomic question).

Chapter 8 looks at the important question of economic growth. In this chapter Mark Setterfield contrasts the neoclassical and Post Keynesian visions of the growth process. For neoclassicals, growth is primarily a supply-side phenomenon. In contrast, Post Keynesians see growth as demand determined and also dependent on past behavior and economic conditions. Post Keynesians, in contrast to neoclassical economists, put path dependence at the foundation of its analysis of growth. What this means in practice is that an economy heading down a bad path, and experiencing high unemployment, may not easily remedy itself and achieve full employment or move to a better growth path. The door is thus open for government policies to spur long-term growth.

Chapter 9 examines the Post Keynesian views on money and inflation. L. Randall Wray explains why Post Keynesians hold that the money supply is determined endogenously, or from within the economic system. It is the demand by firms for money to expand their operations that generates bank loans and a greater money supply. In addition, while inflation is mainly a monetary phenomenon for neoclassical economists, Post Keynesians view inflation as a conflict over the distribution of real output. The appropriate policy solution is thus *not* higher unemployment, but an incomes policy that allows the various claimants to decide on an acceptable distribution of real output. Another useful policy is to develop buffer stocks of important commodities (like oil and labor). When the economy is doing poorly and unemployment becomes a problem, the government needs to buy labor and develop a buffer stock of workers. This will add to both demand and employment. Conversely, when demand is high and inflation threatens, the government must sell its buffer stocks. Throwing these goods on to the market will lower their price and thus reduce inflationary pressures.

In Chapter 10, Steven Pressman examines the role of the state more directly. Keynes *assumed* a certain economic role for the state and advanced a set of policies for the state to enact. However, for all his concern with the real world, he did not address how economic policy would be implemented in the real world. This gap led to several critiques of the Keynesian view of the state, and to a macroeconomic theory which holds that government policy can never improve economic performance. Chapter 10 responds to these critiques and develops a Post Keynesian view of the state. Because people are not always rational, and because they operate in a world of uncertainty, institutions affect individual behavior and economic outcomes. State action becomes important because it can alter behavioral conventions. And without state action, institutional behaviors will keep an economy mired in recession or depression. Appropriate state budget policy is thus necessary for a well-functioning economy.

In Chapter 11 John Smithin looks at international monetary arrangements from a Post Keynesian perspective. Smithin notes that while neoclassical theory tends to support free capital flows and free exchange rates, Post Keynesians have not been enthusiastic about these free-market outcomes. He then sets out a number of different positions held by Post Keynesians regarding how to structure the international monetary order. Smithin notes that although there is no consensus on particulars (some Post Keynesians support fixed exchange rates while others support flexible exchange rates; some support capital controls while others support free capital flows), there is consensus on goals. For all Post Keynesians, any exchange rate policy and any policy on capital flows should contribute to full employment and economic stability.

Finally, in Chapter 12, we look at the future direction for Post Keynesian economics in the twenty-first century. In our view, over the past half century the Post Keynesian viewpoint has been substantially developed at both the methodological and the theoretical level. There is a distinctive Post Keynesian methodology and a Post Keynesian theoretical approach that is both coherent and consistent. However, much work remains to be done at the empirical and the policy level. In particular, Post Keynesians need to set forth clear policy recommendations on key contemporary problems, and they need to make an empirical case for the superiority of both Post Keynesian theory and Post Keynesian policies.

Because *laissez-faire* does not lead to optimal outcomes, activist economic policy is required if real economies are to perform well. Post Keynesians need to develop this policy analysis and make a case for the effectiveness of their policy proposals for the economic challenges now facing us. This is especially important for some of the key economic issues of the early twenty-first century – how to improve productivity growth, the coming retirement (social security) crisis, health care issues, and environmental problems, to name just a few.

References

Arestis, P. (1992) *The Post Keynesian Approach to Economics*, Aldershot: Edward Elgar.

Arestis, P. (1996) "Post-Keynesian Economics: Towards Coherence," *Cambridge Journal of Economics*, 20: 111–35.

Asimakopulas, A. (1971) "The Determinants of Investment in Keynes's Model," *Canadian Journal of Economics*, 4: 382–8.

Asimakopulas, A. (1991) *Keynes's General Theory and Accumulation*, Cambridge: Cambridge University Press.

Davidson, P. (1972) *Money and the Real World*, London: Macmillan.

Davidson, P. (1982) *International Money and the Real World*, London: Macmillan.

Davidson, P. (1994) *Post Keynesian Macroeconomic Theory*, Aldershot: Edward Elgar.

Dunn, S. (2000) "Whither Post Keynesianism," *Journal of Post Keynesian Economics*, 20: 345–64.

Eichner, A.S. (1976) *The Megacorp and Oligopoly*, Cambridge: Cambridge University Press.

Eichner, A.S. (1978) *A Guide to Post Keynesian Economics*, Armonk, NY: M.E. Sharpe.

Friedman, M. (1953) "The Methodology of Positive Economics," in *Essays in Positive Economics*, Chicago: University of Chicago Press, pp. 3–43.

Galbraith, J.K. (1952) *A Theory of Price Control*, Cambridge: Harvard University Press.

Galbraith, J.K. (1967) *The New Industrial State*, Boston: Houghton Mifflin.

Garegnani, P. (1960) *Il Capitale nelle Teorie della Distribuzione*, Milan: Giuffre.

Harcourt, G.C. (1965) "A Two-Sector Model of the Distribution of Income and the Level of Employment in the Short Run," *Economic Record*, 41: 103–17.

Harcourt, G.C. (1972) *Some Cambridge Controversies in the Theory of Capital*, Cambridge: Cambridge University Press.

Harcourt, G.C. and Peter Kenyon (1976) "Pricing and the Investment Decision," *Kyklos*, 29: 449–77.

Holt, R., Rosser, J.B. Jr and Wray, L.R. (1998) "Paul Davidson: The Truest Keynesian?" *Eastern Economic Journal*, 24: 495–506.

Kaldor, N. (1967) *Strategic Factors in Economic Development*, Ithaca: New York State School of Industrial and Labor Relations.

Kaldor, N. (1982) *The Scourge of Monetarism*, Oxford: Oxford University Press.

Keynes, J.M. [1936] (1964) *The General Theory of Employment, Interest and Money*, New York: Harcourt Brace and World.

Lavoie, M. (1992) *Foundations of Post Keynesian Analysis*, Aldershot, UK: Edward Elgar.

Minsky, H. (1982) *Can "It" Happen Again?* Armonk, NY: M.E. Sharpe.

Moore, B.J. (1988) *Horizontalists and Verticalists: The Macroeconomics of Credit Money*, New York: Cambridge University Press.

Pasinetti, L. (1960) "A Mathematical Formulation of the Ricardian System," *Review of Economic Studies*, 27: 78–98.

Pasinetti, L. (1962) "Rate of Profit and Income Distribution in Relation to the Rate of Economic Growth," *Review of Economic Studies*, 29: 267–79.

Pressman, S. (1998) "The Policy Dissent of Nicholas Kaldor," in R.P.F. Holt and S. Pressman (eds.) *Economics and Its Discontents*, Cheltenham: Edward Elgar, pp. 106–18.

Robinson, J. (1933) *The Economics of Imperfect Competition*, London: Macmillan.

Robinson, J. (1980) *Collected Economic Papers*, 5 vols, Cambridge, MA: MIT Press.

Sawyer, M. (1985) *The Economics of Michal Kalecki*, Armonk, NY: M.E. Sharpe.

Sawyer, M. (1998) "The Positive Dissent of Michal Kalecki," in R.P.F. Holt and S. Pressman (eds.) *Economics and Its Discontents*, Cheltenham: Edward Elgar, pp. 119–34.

Sraffa, P. (1926) "The Laws of Return Under Competitive Conditions," *Economic Journal* 36: 535–50.

Sraffa, P. (1960) *The Production of Commodities by Means of Commodities*, Cambridge: Cambridge University Press.

Weintraub, S. (1958) *An Approach to the Theory of Income Distribution*, Philadelphia: Chilton.

Weintraub, S. (1961) *Classical Keynesianism, Monetary Theory and the Price Level*, Philadelphia: Chilton.

Weintraub, S. (1966) *A Keynesian Theory of Employment Growth and Income Distribution*, Philadelphia: Chilton.

Weintraub, S. and Wallich, H. (1978) "A Tax-Based Incomes Policy," in S. Weintraub (ed.) *Keynes, Keynesians and Monetarists*, Philadelphia: University of Pennsylvania Press, pp. 259–80.

2 Post Keynesian methodology

Sheila Dow

Introduction

Methodology is concerned with the choice of methods of analysis, and the means of choosing between competing theories. For neoclassical economists the method of analysis is mathematical formalism, and they choose those theories that predict best. Mathematical formalism is appealing because it makes what is being analyzed clear and precise; it also allows theories to be easily compared. Good theories predict well and become accepted; other theories are bad theories.

One drawback to this view of methodology is that it discourages consideration of alternative schools of thought. Any methodology developed outside the neoclassical framework inevitably fails by neoclassical criteria. It is therefore important that Post Keynesians not just explain their methodology; they must also use methodological arguments to justify considering something broader than neoclassical methodology. Post Keynesian methodology needs to make clear that its approach to economics can be justified, and also make the case that its methodology provides a better understanding of how the economy works.

This chapter discusses what methodology means for Post Keynesian economics and how its views on methodology have developed. For Post Keynesians, methodology is a matter of discussing not only how models are chosen, but also what is meant by empirical assessment and how the real world is understood. Methodology also provides a basis to critique mainstream economics and a mechanism to mark out Post Keynesian territory.

Today, methodologists know that there is no universal set of methodological principles. Each school of thought is characterized by its own methodology; the specification of that methodology comes from inside the school. By observing what Post Keynesians do, the methodologist can rationally reconstruct practice as conforming to a set of methodological principles. These principles can then be discussed and, if need be, questioned or updated.

The next section discusses the philosophical foundations of economic methodology. The third section considers the different aspects of the Post Keynesian methodology and argues that these are mutually compatible. The fourth section considers some unresolved methodological issues. The final section summarizes the Post Keynesian approach to methodology and discusses some of its policy implications.

Philosophical foundations

Early methodological statements of Post Keynesianism emphasized the importance of historical time, and the theoretical implications of taking historical time seriously. Key figures, such as Robinson (1978) and Kaldor (1972), emphasized that conducting economic analysis in terms of historical time means that we have to do without equilibrium in the mainstream sense of the term. They questioned conventional supply and demand analysis (which requires pure competition and the independence of supply and demand) because it did not correspond to real world conditions. This raised issues about what types of lack of realism we are prepared to accept (all theory being in some sense unrealistic).

Neither Robinson nor Kaldor was explicit about methodology in the traditional sense. They focused on theoretical differences rather than questioning the whole basis for theory appraisal. At that time, the field of methodology was dominated by Popper's ([1934] 1950) ideas about testing hypotheses. Reference to "the facts" was central. According to Popper, while confirming instances could not prove a theory true, contradiction by the facts could prove it false. Theory testing should thus be designed to narrow the range of what was true by eliminating what could be shown to be false. Implicit in Popper was the view that empirical testing was the best way to appraise a theory.

Friedman (1953) reduced the issue of empirical testing to a question of predictive success. The structure of a theory and the realism of its assumptions were not important. Instead, we should choose that theory which predicts best. It was not just Post Keynesians who reacted against such a methodology by arguing for the merits of explanation as an alternative to prediction and a means of generating better predictions. And it was not just Post Keynesians who argued for more realistic theories.

But the critique had particular force for Post Keynesians, for whom the starting point of theory was the nature of the real world. Post Keynesians thought it crucial that there be some correspondence between a theory and the real world, something that Friedman denied.

Meanwhile, the philosophy of science was undergoing a major transformation. Previously, the goal had been to identify the best method for science, and the best way to choose theories. But, drawing on the work of Thomas Kuhn (1962), in the 1960s philosophers of science began to raise questions about whether it was possible to identify one best method of theory appraisal. Kuhn observed, through a study of the history of science, that theory choice was not a simple matter of testing a theory against the empirical evidence, as suggested by traditional philosophy of science. Instead, science proceeded within communities of scientists, each with a shared paradigm.

A paradigm consists of a disciplinary matrix based on a particular world view and communicated by exemplars (Kuhn, 1974). The world view determines core beliefs about the nature of the subject matter and the questions asked, whereas the disciplinary matrix provides the theoretical and empirical tools used to answer these questions. There are no universal, external criteria by which to judge which is the best paradigm. Each paradigm has its own set of criteria for theory selection, and there is no basis for applying these criteria to other paradigms.

In practice, scientists operate within a scientific community, so that the range of world views, and thus paradigms, is limited. Within each social grouping of scientists, conventions are shared about how to proceed. Contrary empirical evidence is not sufficient grounds for giving up a paradigm; evidence is understood differently depending on the paradigm. For example, a paradigm that precludes involuntary unemployment would interpret high unemployment as evidence of high voluntary unemployment. There is no conflict with the presumption of market clearing.

Based on the work of Kuhn, Dow (1985) argued that economic schools of thought are most effectively identified at the methodological level as paradigms. Methodological differences had to be understood if communication between schools of thought was to succeed. A corollary of this is that ideology is part of the world view that defines a school of thought and its methodological principles.

Kuhn thus opened the door for developing a methodology that would explain the Post Keynesian world view and its disciplinary matrix as a coherent whole. These methodological underpinnings were expressed in different ways by different Post Keynesians. The next section explores some of these specifications.

Post Keynesian methodology

Joan Robinson (1975) worked with Keynes at Cambridge and was perhaps the first to use the term "Post Keynesian." She highlighted the role of ideology in theory; but she also reflected the times by taking the stand that the ideology of different schools of thought could be separated from theory, so that, as long as ideological differences were made explicit, arguments could be settled by reason (Salanti, 1996).[1]

Paul Davidson (1972) continued to highlight methodological issues and the role of ideology. He emphasized the significance of conducting analysis in terms of historical time, rather than the logical time used by orthodox theory. Historical time is distinctive in being irreversible – something precluded by most orthodox analyses. Davidson also highlighted the uncertainty of expectations with respect to an unknown future. If economic relationships were not determinate and timeless, it was impossible to analyze equilibrium in the same way as orthodox theory. So equilibrium for Post Keynesians came to refer to stable states, rather than the market clearing and satisfaction of expectations that characterize the orthodox concept of equilibrium. Relying on this foundation, Davidson (1972) built a theory of money in historical time. It showed money to be integral to economic relations because of its role as refuge from uncertainty.

Alfred Eichner (1978), also in the US, provided the first general account of Post Keynesian economics. He too put great emphasis on its methodological distinctiveness. In particular, he emphasized that a methodology emphasizing historical time will have to be applied to industrial structures that are not perfectly competitive. This means that the conditions for orthodox supply and demand analysis will not be met. (For example, the supply curve is not defined in the absence of perfect competition.)

In the UK, Victoria Chick (1983) drew attention to the distinctive methodological aspects of *The General Theory*, and argued that understanding the methodology of *The General Theory* was necessary for understanding its economics. Keynes focused on a monetary production economy, rather than a real exchange economy, because he was trying to understand such an economic system. This led to a focus on time, uncertainty, and money. This, in turn, required a combination of partial and general analysis, including his use of different time horizons and his notion of equilibrium as a state of rest where no one had the power to effect change (even if they had the desire to do so). From all this Keynes could explain unemployment equilibrium.

Reissue of the *Treatise on Probability* (Keynes, 1973) made clear the philosophy behind Keynes's methodology. In the *Treatise*, Keynes developed a theory of how we (as economists and as economic agents) establish reasoned grounds for belief under conditions of uncertainty. Following Hume ([1739–40] 1978), Keynes thought that, as mere humans, we could not know with any certainty the causal forces underpinning complex relationships. We could only draw on experience, the human faculties, reason (as opposed to rationality), and intuition. Hume emphasized the importance of beliefs. Our belief system, in turn, reflects our social nature, so that social convention plays a part. Keynes (1937) talked of people relying on conventional opinion of what would happen in financial markets because they lacked any other guidance. The remaining gap is filled by what Hume termed "the imagination" and what Keynes termed "intuition." These are combined with reason and conventional judgment in order to form a view on the basis of available evidence.

A rich literature on the philosophy of Keynes followed, which demonstrated the coherent methodological underpinnings of his economics (building on Lawson and Pesaran, 1985; Carabelli, 1988; O'Donnell, 1989; Davis, 1994). There is still much debate over whether, at what level, and how far Keynes changed his mind over time. Particularly controversial is the understanding of Keynes's view on the organicism (interrelatedness) of individuals and of social systems (i.e. the nature of the subject matter as a basis for the design of theory). But whether or not Keynes started as an atomist, there is general agreement that he ended as an organicist.

Although much methodological discussion focused on Keynes, Post Keynesian economics was originally much broader in scope. The early development of Post Keynesianism in North America, and in the Trieste summer school, included a range of non-mainstream approaches (Lee, 1998). While aiding in the institutional development of Post Keynesianism, the resulting pluralism (in the absence of explicit methodological justification) created difficulties when it came to classifying Post Keynesianism in a positive sense, rather than as a critique of the mainstream. An early definitive account of Post

Keynesianism (Hamouda and Harcourt, 1988) presented it in terms of three strands (following the traditions of Keynes, Sraffa, and Kalecki/Robinson). This raised the issue of whether Post Keynesianism was methodologically coherent and whether there was a Post Keynesian methodology.

Several attempts have been made to identify the methodological principles implicit in Post Keynesian economics.

For Davidson, methodology requires a concern with realism, also taking into account the real world implications of historical time when doing economics. Davidson (1994) went on to develop an account of Post Keynesian methodology that emphasizes its generalizing nature. He understood Keynes as offering a general approach, of which neoclassical economics was a special case. He characterized Post Keynesianism as rejecting three neo-classical axioms – the axiom of the neutrality of money, the axiom of gross substitution, and the ergodic axiom. By rejecting these axioms, Davidson argues, Keynes was able to develop a more general theoretical framework that could be applied to particular circumstances.

Money is crucial because there is no close substitute for it and because it is not neutral (i.e. it affects the real world) in a world of uncertainty. An asset with a relatively stable and certain value is necessary for times of high uncertainty and, more generally, as the denominator of contracts.

Systems are ergodic if their structure remains stable over time, so that extrapolation from the past is a good guide to the future. Ergodic systems lend themselves to mathematical representation and econometric testing, as in orthodox economics. Non-ergodic systems imply uncertainty in the real world, so that formal equation systems cannot capture the complexity of reality. Put another way, non-ergodic systems are those where historical time generates structural change, whereas in ergodic systems historical time can be represented satisfactorily by logical time. Some economic relations may be ergodic. For these, neoclassical methodology is appropriate, but this requires special justification as an exception to the norm of non-ergodicity. Thus, while not rejecting mainstream economics, Davidson contains it (Chick, 1995a), arguing that it is only a good theory for special circumstances.

Lawson (1994) is even more skeptical about neoclassical methodology. He advocates that Post Keynesians adopt critical realist foundations. Critical realism holds that the purpose of science is to uncover causal structures. For the critical realist, what we observe as empirical events is only a surface manifestation of the real underlying causal forces that we cannot directly observe. Consequently, the orthodox focus on econometric testing of models is limited because it only looks at surface characteristics. A critical realist account of inflation would seek to identify the forces at work underlying both changes in monetary conditions and changes in the general price level, rather than specific predictions about how monetary changes affect the general price level.

For critical realists, social systems are regarded as complex, structured, and transformable. This corresponds with Keynes's understanding of social systems as organic and Davidson's understanding of them as non-ergodic.

Understanding the social structure is the first step to transforming it. This supports the reformist stance of Post Keynesian economics.

What follows is open-system theorizing. In an open system one does not know all the relevant variables. Post Keynesians understand the economy as an open system. The social system, with its institutions and conventions, evolves and human agency can generate surprises. Open systems can also be transformed by human agency. In contrast, mainstream economics views the real world as a closed system. This view justifies its representation by a single formal model that can be tested empirically with econometric techniques. Relevant variables are fully specified, and they are used to analyze a wide variety of contexts over time and space.

The notion of an open system approach has numerous affinities with the idea of a Babylonian mode of thought. Dow (1985; 1996) developed this latter notion to capture a different way of understanding complex systems. Like critical realism, it does this by approaching a question from a range of angles and using a variety of methods (in contrast with the mathematical method of orthodox economics). This approach also corresponds to Keynes's (1937) view on how we establish reasonable grounds for belief under uncertainty – knowledge is built up by means of conventions and intuition as well as ordinary logic applied to all available evidence. It also provides a coherent rationale for a methodology that employs a range of methods, taking various starting points.

The Babylonian mode of thought has been accused of advocating "anything goes," similar to postmodernist ideas and the rhetoric approach, which seem to be putting forward the view that there is really no methodology. However, this characterization is not accurate. The Babylonian approach occupies a middle ground, between one set of rules and no rules. It advocates a set of methodological principles corresponding to a set of schools of thought. Rather than the pure pluralism of postmodernism, this is a pluralism modified and structured according to principles peculiar to Post Keynesianism (see Dow, 1997). Critical realism also occupies a middle ground, recognizing the impediments to establishing truth with respect to a complex social system. The objective is to seek, as far as possible, true knowledge. But recognizing that this is an unachievable goal, a variety of approaches to establishing (fallible) knowledge becomes necessary.

Chick (1995b) further develops the idea of Post Keynesianism as a distinctive way of thinking. This approach stresses the primacy of the problem at hand for deciding on the theory and method to use. Like critical realism, the goal is to transform society, and, like the Babylonian approach, different aspects of the social system are analyzed in different ways, depending on the context.

While there have been several accounts of Post Keynesian methodology, sufficient common ground exists to identify something approaching a consensus position.

The general methodological approach is an open system approach, involving collections of partial analyses that aim to build up a (fallible) knowledge of different aspects of the socioeconomic system. Rather than relying on a single, formal method, a range of methods are employed (formal, institutional, and historical, for example) that draw on different types of evidence (case studies or published data series, depending on the problem at hand). As a corollary, there is no single set of axioms from which all theories are drawn.

It should not be surprising that Post Keynesian methodology has developed in the same way that methodology suggests theory should develop – following different chains of reasoning, taking different starting-points (depending on context), but unified by a shared vision of reality (see Dow, 1990). This vision includes a focus on production rather than exchange, a focus on imperfect competition, and a focus on distributional questions. A further important element of the view of methodology outlined above is that methodology itself is an evolving body of knowledge. Debate on these foundations therefore continues.

Unresolved issues

As we noted above, Post Keynesian methodology is still evolving; so the above summary should be regarded as only provisional. In fact, changing methodological principles may be seen as one aspect of an open system. Several issues remain under debate and comprise part of an evolving Post Keynesian methodology.

First, there is the question of the role of econometrics. Lawson (1997) takes a strong position against using econometrics on the grounds that the conditions for its application are virtually never met (namely, that the subject matter conforms to a closed system). But many Post Keynesians find that econometrics is a useful tool for understanding the real economic world. There are several ways to deal with this issue. One possibility is to give up critical realism; another is to give up econometrics. But intermediate possibilities are being explored (see Mearman, 1998) for justifying the use of econometrics under certain carefully specified conditions.

Another unresolved methodological issue concerns expectations. There is a broad spectrum of opinion here. At one extreme are followers of Shackle (1972), who emphasize the subjectivity of expectations. At the other extreme are those who analyze expectations in terms of reason. Finally, some Post Keynesians choose to give expectations and uncertainty a very minor role. For example, horizontalists focus on credit creation and downplay the relevance of liquidity preference theory, which is built on the view that money takes its role from the existence of uncertainty (see Cottrell, 1994, for a review of Post Keynesian monetary theory which explains the different approaches). Since Post Keynesians stress the importance of uncertainty, a Post Keynesian theory giving diminished attention to uncertainty may raise problems of inconsistency. This is currently a matter under active debate.

The importance of uncertainty reflects a more general difference of opinion between the Sraffian strand of Post Keynesian economics and the rest, since Sraffian long-run analysis explicitly abstracts from uncertainty in order to identify structural tendencies. It is difficult, therefore, to reconcile the methodology specified above with the Sraffian approach. Indeed, it has even been suggested that attempts to identify the Sraffian approach with Post Keynesianism should be discontinued (see Roncaglia, 1995).

This issue raises a more general issue, which is the relation between Post Keynesian economics and other non-mainstream approaches. To the extent that all share an open-system approach to economics, there is much common ground. The literature demonstrates the fertility of this common ground, with ideas bouncing back and forth between Post Keynesians and other non-mainstream economists. Neo-Austrians, Institutionalists, Marxians and Post Keynesians, for example, can profit from reading each other's work. But what they make of it will depend on the school of thought to which they belong.

Socially and institutionally, such cooperation helps build knowledge and understanding. Nevertheless, it is useful to have an idea of the "representative" Post Keynesian. Kuhn's idea of scientific revolutions did not fit economics well, because ideas change gradually and many economists fail to fit neatly into categories. Indeed, many non-mainstream economists prefer not to take on the label of a particular school and like operating in these middle grounds. But the idea of a paradigm or school of thought is still a useful organizing principle, reflecting a set of ideas that guide practice within an otherwise uncharted open-system approach. Just as conventions provide stable reference points for economic activity, institutionalized schools of thought provide stable reference points for economic analysis.

Conclusion and policy implications

One of the most important contributions that methodology can make is to spell out how economists appraise theories. Post Keynesians embrace a multi-strand and multi-method approach to questions and issues, depending on the particular context. They justify such an approach as a good way of building up (fallible) knowledge of the real world.

This approach is coherent because Post Keynesians share a common view of the world. This view determines the kind of questions asked, the methods used, and points to the underlying purpose of economics as a means of employing policy to improve economic performance. It is important that there be alternatives to the single, formal method of neo-classical economics and that these alternatives can be fully justified by philosophical and methodological foundations. Post Keynesian economics provides such an alternative.

The approach is also practical because Post Keynesian thought is well suited for applying economics to policy issues. Policy-making requires an understanding of underlying structure so that we can understand the effects of policies applied to a changing structure, and also the effects of policies designed to change structure itself. The advantages of neoclassical formalism (namely the precision and certainty of the conclusions) depend, among other things, on the *ceteris paribus* clause being satisfied. What Post Keynesianism gives up in terms of precision and certainty, it more than makes up for in its understanding of the causal mechanisms underlying the real economy and its ability to draw on a range of methods.

Post Keynesian methodology is based on its particular world view and leads to its distinctive policy approach. This approach has five main elements.

1   The economic process is seen as being ordered to a considerable degree because of institutions and conventional behavior, rather than because of market coordination. However, there is always the potential for disorder due to creative, profit-seeking behavior and the revision of expectations under conditions of uncertainty. Economic structures are not inherently stable, either because institutions and conventions may change, or because expectations may change discretely or the degree of uncertainty itself may change.

2   There are inevitable limits to knowledge. This means that, in general, knowledge of economic relations is held with uncertainty. Uncertainty is the norm since social systems transform themselves unpredictably.

3   Money is the social institution devised to address uncertainty. It serves as the denominator of labor and debt contracts, and allows capitalist economies to function.

4   There is a focus on production rather than exchange as the driving force in the economy. Demand and supply are understood to be interdependent, and imperfect competition is seen as the normal structure in product and factor markets.

5   Income distribution and, more generally, the distribution of economic power are perceived as significant social issues for economics to address.[2]

Notes

1   She persisted in attempting to communicate ideas with orthodox economists in spite of differing methodologies. The lack of understanding among mainstream economists of the feasibility of different methodological starting points led to the confusions of the Capital Controversies; see Dow (1980).

2   This chapter has benefited from comments and suggestions from Geoff Harcourt and the editors.

References

Carabelli, A. (1988) *On Keynes's Method*, London: Macmillan.

Chick, V. (1983) *Macroeconomics After Keynes*, Oxford: Philip Allan.

Chick, V. (1995a) "Order out of Chaos in Economics?" in S.C. Dow and J. Hillard (eds.), *Keynes, Knowledge and Uncertainty*, Aldershot: Elgar, pp. 25–42.

Chick, V. (1995b) "Is There a Case for Post Keynesian Economics?" *Scottish Journal of Political Economy*, 42: 20–36.

Cottrell, A. (1994) "Post Keynesian Monetary Economics," *Cambridge Journal of Economics*, 18: 587–605.

Davidson, P. (1972) *Money and the Real World*, London: Macmillan.

Davidson, P. (1994) *Post Keynesian Macroeconomic Theory*, Aldershot: Edward Elgar.

Davis, J.B. (1994) *Keynes's Philosophical Development*, Cambridge: Cambridge University Press.

Dow, S.C. (1980) "Methodological Morality in the Capital Controversies," *Journal of Post Keynesian Economics*, 2: 368–80.

Dow, S.C. (1985) *Macroeconomic Thought: A Methodological Approach*, Oxford: Blackwell.

Dow, S.C. (1990) "Post Keynesianism as Political Economy: A Methodological Discussion," *Review of Political Economy*, 2: 345–58.

Dow, S.C. (1996) *The Methodology of Macroeconomic Thought*, Aldershot: Edward Elgar.

Dow, S.C. (1997) "Methodological Pluralism and Pluralism of Method," in A. Salanti and E. Screpanti (eds.) *Pluralism in Economics: Theory, History and Methodology*, Aldershot: Edward Elgar, pp. 89–99.

Eichner, A.S. (1978) *A Guide to Post Keynesian Economics*, London: Macmillan.

Friedman, M. (1953) "The Methodology of Positive Economics," in *Essays in Positive Economics*, Chicago: Chicago University Press, pp. 3–34.

Hamouda, O.F. and Harcourt G.C. (1989) "Post-Keynesianism: From Criticism to Coherence?" in J. Pheby (ed.) *New Directions in Post-Keynesian Economics*, Aldershot: Edward Elgar, pp. 1–34.

Hume, D. [1739–40] (1978) *A Treatise of Human Nature*, K. Selby-Bigge and P.H. Nedditch (eds.) 2nd edn, Oxford: Clarendon.

Kaldor, N. (1972) "The Irrelevance of Equilibrium Economics," *Economic Journal*, 82: 1237–55.

Keynes, J.M. (1937) "The General Theory of Employment," *Quarterly Journal of Economics*, 51: 209–23.

Keynes, J.M. (1973) *A Treatise on Probability*, *The Collected Writings of John Maynard Keynes*, vol. VIII, London: Macmillan.

Kuhn, T.S. (1962) *The Structure of Scientific Revolutions*, Chicago: Chicago University Press.

Kuhn, T.S. (1974) "Second Thoughts on Paradigms," in F. Suppe (ed.) *The Structure of Scientific Theories*, Urbana: University of Illinois Press, pp. 459–82.

Lawson, T. (1994) "The Nature of Post Keynesianism and its Links to other Traditions: A Realist Perspective," *Journal of Post Keynesian Economics*, 16: 503–38.

Lawson, T. (1997) *Economics and Reality*, London: Routledge.

Lawson, T. and Pesaran, M.H. (eds.) (1985) *Keynes's Economics: Methodological Issues*, London: Croom Helm.

Lee, F. (1998) *Alfred Eichner, Joan Robinson and the Founding of Post Keynesian Economics*, de Montfort University mimeo.

Mearman, A. (1998) *Keynes, Realism and Econometrics*, paper presented to the Third Annual Postgraduate Economics Conference, Leeds, November.

O'Donnell, R.M. (1989) *Keynes: Philosophy, Economics and Politics*, London: Macmillan.

Popper, K. [1934] (1950) *The Logic of Scientific Discovery*, New York: Harper and Row.

Robinson, J. (1975) "Introduction," in *Collected Papers*, vol. 2, Oxford: Blackwell, pp. iii–xii.

Robinson, J. (1978) "History versus Equilibrium," in *Contributions to Modern Economics*, Oxford: Blackwell, pp. 126–36.

Roncaglia, A. (1995) "On the Compatibility between Keynes's and Sraffa's Viewpoints on Output Levels," in G.C. Harcourt, A. Roncaglia and R. Rowley (eds.) *Income and Employment in Theory and Practice*, New York: St Martin's Press, pp. 111–25.

Salanti, A. (1996) "Joan Robinson's Changing View on Method: A Tentative Appraisal," in M.C. Marcuzo, L.L. Pasinetti and A. Roncaglia (eds.) *The Economics of Joan Robinson*, London: Routledge, pp. 285–99.

Shackle, G.L.S. (1972) *Epistemics and Economics*, Cambridge: Cambridge University Press.

3   Pricing

Marc Lavoie

Introduction

Pricing in mainstream economics seems to be rather simple. For competitive firms no decision needs to be made; price is set by the market. Competitive firms then decide how much to produce by equating this price to marginal cost. In the case of a monopoly things are barely more complicated; the firm follows two simple rules – equate marginal revenue to marginal cost, and charge as much as demand warrants.

In both cases prices clear the market; everything produced gets sold. Moreover, prices reflect the scarcity of each good. If demand rises, prices rise. This follows from the assumption of diminishing returns; higher outputs induce higher marginal costs, and hence higher prices.

Post Keynesians view pricing as much more complex. Even if firms want to maximize profits, they only have approximate information about demand schedules; and knowledge about consumers is costly to obtain and uncertain. Firms also operate in a world of monopolistic competition and oligopolies. The environment is one of interdependencies; at any time rivals, actual or potential, may change their behavior and employ new strategies. In such an environment, short-run profit maximization is not possible to achieve. Moreover, profit maximization is an inappropriate goal for firms that strive to survive and want some power over their economic environment. Finally, the goals of firms and of their managers are multidimensional; as circumstances change, the weight given to various goals is revised and some goals need to be modified. In this complex world, business executives adopt simple rules, based on accessible data, that allow them to monitor financial results.

Cost-plus pricing is one of these rules. Cost-plus pricing means that firms fix prices based on some measure of costs, rather than as a reaction to demand fluctuations. As John Kenneth Galbraith (1952: 18) succinctly put it, pricing by custom is "an indispensable simplification of what otherwise would be an inordinately complex task." It allows firms to fix prices according to the purpose at hand.

Cost-plus pricing prevails in most product and service markets. The only exceptions are those industries where output is produced in batches, as in some areas of agriculture, or where output is not easily reproducible, as in the art market. In these cases, supplies cannot be quickly increased and adjustments are made through prices. In other industries, short-run fluctuations in demand have little effect on prices. An important feature of these markets is that their output is readily reproducible: if more refrigerators are needed, more refrigerators will be forthcoming. Firms usually operate with spare capacity because they want to respond quickly to any surge of demand or change in its composition, thus avoiding the loss of market share.

A related characteristic of markets based on cost-plus pricing is that marginal and average variable costs are approximately constant, while average total costs generally decrease. Greater demand therefore generates no increase in unit costs and creates no inducement for prices to rise. On the contrary, large volumes encourage firms to set lower prices, or at least not increase prices. Because of falling unit costs, there is no optimal firm size. Markets are dominated by a few large oligopolistic firms, around which sometimes gravitate a multitude of smaller firms that try to differentiate their product and acquire some local monopolistic power. More often than not, the large oligopolies will be price leaders, while the smaller firms adjust their cost margins to the prices set by industry leaders.

Varieties of cost-plus pricing

Cost-plus pricing comes in several variants, but these all share a few salient characteristics. First, prices are not indices of scarcity; rather they reflect costs of production. Hence, prices are cost-coverers and not resource-allocators. Second, entrepreneurs fix prices based on what they consider to be normal costs and then add a markup or costing margin. Third, prices are reproductive prices. They are not set as a one-shot profit-maximizing affair; rather, prices are set within a framework of repetitive transactions with purchasers and with the intent of financing future growth (Lee, 1985: 209). Fourth, prices are not market clearing. Costing margins are added *ex ante*, before the firm can find out what their costs or what the demand conditions really are. Prices are administered and are set before transactions take place. A large share of costs comes from intermediate inputs, whose prices may not be known with certainty when firms set their own prices. This interdependence of prices is another key feature of Post Keynesian pricing.[1]

The simplest cost-plus pricing procedure is the *Kaleckian markup approach*. With markup pricing, prices are assumed to depend on unit prime costs, also called "unit direct costs." These are direct labor costs, and the cost of intermediate goods and raw materials. Although there are subtle differences between prime costs and variable costs (variable costs include overhead labor costs, the salaries of supervisors, which could be avoided if a plant were to be closed down), for most purposes one can take variable, direct, and prime costs as synonyms. Since many authors assume that unit prime costs are constant up to or near full capacity, and since most firms try to avoid operating beyond full capacity, the level of capacity utilization at which these unit prime costs are computed is of little importance. Markup pricing assumes that a gross margin is added to unit prime costs, thus yielding the price of the good.[2]

While markup pricing remains quite popular among Post Keynesian macroeconomists, some authors (notably Lee, 1985; 1994) have argued that markup procedures are becoming less prevalent as a result of increasingly sophisticated accounting techniques. Whereas in the past, accountants had only rough estimates of unit fixed costs or of overhead costs (including depreciation costs), this is no longer the case. Most firms, large firms in particular, have accurate estimates of unit overhead costs and can attribute to each branch or product the overhead costs incurred.

A second approach to cost-plus pricing, full-cost pricing, was first presented by Hall and Hitch (1939). Using this approach, firms fix prices by taking into account all their costs and not just direct costs. The full-cost approach depends on *actual* unit costs.[3] But since unit costs usually decline up to full capacity, full-cost pricing fell into disrepute because it meant that prices had to fall with rising production. As Robinson (1977: 11) notes, "the old full cost doctrine ... appeared to hold that prices of manufactures ... fall when demand increases because overheads are spread over a larger output." This seemed too surprising to be accepted. In addition, full-cost pricing meant that actual unit costs (prime costs plus overhead costs) had to be known in advance, something thought to be impossible.

The pricing method now accepted is normal-cost pricing, described by Andrews (1949), Brunner (1952), and Andrews and Brunner (1975). Normal-cost pricing emphasizes that firms fix prices by adding a costing margin to unit costs that have been computed at some normal level of output (Lee *et al.*, 1986: 24). Hence prices depend on some conventional measure of costs, the normal or standard cost.

Andrews (1949) presumed a gross costing margin was added to unit direct costs, assessed at some normal output. Andrews and Brunner (1975) recognized, however, that many larger firms would fix prices by adding a net costing margin to total average costs, estimated at normal output. More recently, normal-cost pricing has become associated with the latter rather than with the former view (Rowthorn, 1981: n. 4; Bhaduri, 1986: 76; Lee, 1994). Normal-cost pricing in its modern incarnation thus takes into account both direct and overhead costs, as in the full-cost approach, but computes unit costs at some conventional level of output.[4]

Obviously, if actual unit costs are changing with output levels (in particular, total average costs usually decline with increased output), firms cannot know in advance what unit costs will be. Normal cost must thus be computed for some normal level of output, or some normal level of capacity utilization. Thus, to a certain extent, assessed unit costs are the result of a convention. Costing procedures are facilitated when some trade association sets these procedures, for instance the standard degree of utilization of current capacity that might be used to compute unit overhead costs. Managers need not know the value of unit costs for all output levels. They only need this value for the normal level of output. In that sense, the exact shape of the various cost curves does not matter; and whether unit direct costs are constant or not becomes immaterial (Lee, 1994: 314).

A variant of the normal-cost approach is target-return pricing. This procedure was identified by Kaplan *et al.* (1958) in their study of large firms, but was also found to be used by a majority of smaller firms (Shipley, 1981: 430). In the target-return procedure, prices are set (given unit direct and indirect costs) to yield a target rate of profit on the capital assets of the company whenever sales correspond to the output produced at the standard rate of capacity utilization. As Lanzillotti (1958: 923) puts it, "margins added to standard costs are designed to produce the target profit rate on investment, assuming standard volume to be the long-run average rate of plant utilization."[5] Target-return pricing is thus the most sophisticated approach, for accountants must have a precise idea of the worth of capital or of the value of newly built plants.

Target-return pricing is also close to the Sraffian approach to prices, or what Nell (1988: 195) calls "benchmark prices." In the canonical Sraffian model, which constitutes the main alternative to mainstream theories of relative prices, it is assumed that best-practice technological coefficients are calculated at standard levels of capacity utilization, and the rates of profit that are imposed upon fixed capital (or variable capital) are assumed to be uniform across industries. With non-uniform rates of profit, which correspond to the differentiated target rates of return of each firm or industry, and assuming that the technological coefficients are those of the firms that act as price-leaders, the Sraffian multisector price model becomes the relative prices version of the target-return pricing approach.[6]

Boggio (1992) has analyzed the properties of target-return pricing models within a system-wide model. His conclusion is that in these target-return pricing models the convergence of relative prices towards constant values requires few assumptions, in contrast to the conditions required to obtain convergence in standard Sraffian models. Many Post Keynesians, however, dispute the relevance of such studies, since convergence requires a large number of periods, during which time the assumed constant data set (production conditions and target rates of return) will likely change (Lee, 1994).

Since these various cost-plus pricing procedures are quite similar one may wonder which one is best. One answer is to be eclectic. Lee (1998: Ch. 12) constructs a multi-sector model, which he calls the empirical pricing model, with a mix of different pricing procedures: some industries relying on a markup approach, others on various specifications of the normal-cost approach and so on. Most macroeconomists prefer the markup approach because its simplicity allows them to tackle complex macro questions without the mathematics becoming impeded by a complicated pricing procedure. It is possible, however, to construct and run macroeconomic models using target-return pricing procedures, and some macroeconomists have done this, sometimes yielding results that can be distinguished from models based on simple markups (Lavoie, 1996, Lavoie and Ramírez-Gastón; 1997). This is particularly recommended for economies dominated by large corporations, since we know that they have the accounting resources to set net costing margins over standard average costs. Overall, however, the markup pricing procedure, with a gross costing margin set over unit direct costs, has been the most popular with Post Keynesian writers.

Determinants of the markup

While Post Keynesians have long endorsed cost-plus pricing, mainstream economists have recently begun to make use of markup pricing. Mainstream authors using this rule of thumb usually point out that a markup over unit variable costs is consistent with profit maximization – the markup depends on the elasticity of demand and is set to equate marginal cost and marginal revenue. This interpretation can also be found in some earlier works of Kalecki and has been endorsed by Cowling (1982). On this view markup pricing appears to be profit maximization under conditions of imperfect competition, in a trial-and-error disguise.

There are two responses to this claim. First, a number of authors have pointed out that demand elasticities computed in empirical studies are inconsistent with this profit-maximizing interpretation of markup pricing. In particular, Koutsoyiannis (1984) found that for most industries the price-elasticity of demand is below one. This implies that marginal revenue is negative, which contradicts the hypothesis of profit maximization, for marginal costs cannot be negative. Second, accounting studies and economic surveys have shown that the most frequent pricing procedure is normal-cost pricing. But normal-cost pricing, in its modern incarnation, takes unit fixed costs or unit overhead costs into account, and not just marginal or variable costs. Normal cost-pricing and target-return pricing are thus incompatible with profit-maximizing neoclassical theories, since the latter presume that overhead costs or fixed costs play no role in the determination of prices.

If the markup does not depend on profit-maximization considerations, what does determine it? The target-return pricing approach offers the clearest answer to this question. Given unit variable costs, the markup over these direct costs will be higher, the higher the unit fixed costs. These may be broken down into fixed labor costs and fixed capital costs. The latter depend on the rate of capital depreciation, the target rate of profit, and the value of capital per unit of output or per unit of capacity output upon which this target rate of profit is applied. The higher the capital-to-capacity ratio, or the higher the incremental capital-to-capacity ratio (when only new additions to capacity are taken into account), the higher the markup over unit direct costs (Eichner, 1987: Ch. 6).

While there can be little disagreement on the relevance of the capital-to-capacity ratio, the determinants of the target rate of return are more controversial.[7] Post Keynesians have offered three different answers.

A first answer is that the target rate of return is the normal rate of profit that entrepreneurs can hope to achieve as a result of competition among themselves and the power struggle involving labor. The more concentrated the industry, and the less powerful the labor organizations linked to the industry, the higher the normal rate of profit for the industry. Fear of entry by new competitors is thus a major determinant of the target rate of return (Sylos Labini, 1962; Andrews, 1949). If capitalists identify profit rate differentials, and if they can enter and exit industries at will, these differentials should vanish. But since some degree of monopoly can usually be sustained, profit differentials can last for prolonged periods of time and hence be reflected in cost margins. Cost margins thus reflect class struggle and/or concentration ratios.

A second answer, which was quite popular when the first *Guide to Post-Keynesian Economics* came out, is that the target rate of return results from a compromise between two forces. On the one hand, to attract new customers, get rid of high-cost competitors, and forestall the entry of new rivals, firms would like the target rate to be as low as possible. On the other hand, capital accumulation cannot be sustained without profits and retained earnings (Steindl, 1952; Eichner, 1987; Wood, 1975; Kaldor, 1985; Capoglu, 1991). As Harcourt and Kenyon (1976) put it, pricing depends on the investment decisions of the firm; greater investment and future growth requires higher prices now. Because there is no optimal firm size, the current and future size of a firm depends on its success in innovating and marketing on the one hand, and on its access to finance for expanding capacity on the other hand. These opposing forces determine the target rate of return. For a given retention ratio, a higher expected secular growth rate should thus induce a higher target rate of return and hence higher costing margins.

This line of thought is consistent with the Cambridge growth models developed by Robinson and Kaldor in the 1950s. In these models, higher growth rates were accompanied by higher realized profit rates – a result of the higher profit margins generated by the improved demand conditions. Within an oligopolistic framework, the higher profit margins are not the result of demand and supply forces in the goods market; rather, they arise from the decisions of the price leaders about costing margins, on the basis of the improved prospects with regard to the secular growth rate.

A third explanation of the target rate of return arose over the last fifteen years, and has been mainly endorsed by a group of Sraffian authors, following suggestions made by Sraffa and Garegnani (Pivetti, 1985). They argue that the target rate of return, or what they call the "normal rate of profit," is determined largely by the real rate of interest that arises from the monetary regime of the central bank. The normal rate of profit is made up of two components – the rate of interest that needs to be paid to lenders, and the net entrepreneurial premium, which is a kind of liquidity premium, designed to compensate for the trouble and risk of engaging in entrepreneurial activity. While the entrepreneurial premium will vary from industry to industry, the rate of interest will be the same for all industries. High real interest rates, as existed during most of the 1980s and 1990s, would thus lead to higher target rates of return. Simply put, interest payments are seen as a cost to the firm, a cost that is incorporated into the target rate of return. Besides being held by

Sraffian authors, this view can also be found in Kaldor (1982: 63), who believed that "interest costs are passed on in higher prices in much the same way as wage costs," and Harrod (1973: 111), who thought that "sustained low rates of interest will presumably in the long run reduce the normal rate of profit."

Of course, there is no reason why we should not try to incorporate all three views of the determinants of the target rate of return into a single model (Lavoie, 1992: 109–18).

Important complications

It is evident that different plants and different firms in the same industry face different unit costs. Some firms are less efficient than others because they have older plants, which do not incorporate the latest technological developments. None the less, for products that can be compared, one usually observes fairly homogeneous prices. There is nothing surprising about identical prices under highly competitive conditions. Under oligopolistic conditions prices will tend to be identical because customers who discover that they got a bad deal would most certainly change suppliers (Andrews, 1949).

Since prices are identical while unit costs are not, all firms cannot entertain the same markup or the same target rate of return. There must be some price leader, or a group of leading firms, that sets the price for the industry. The price leader position can stem from greater market share or product innovation, or because its unit costs set the industry standard. Other firms (the followers) must adjust their cost margins and prices to the standard set by the price leaders. Kalecki (1971: 45) has long emphasized that the price set by an individual firm depends both on its unit costs and on the prices of other firms. Similarly, Andrews and Brunner (1975: 31) point out that firms with higher than average costs will not be able to set costing margins that provide a normal profit. The consequence of these cost differentials, as both Steindl (1952) and Kaldor (1985) stressed, is that price competition proceeds by reducing the profits of high-cost firms, thus impeding their ability to finance research and development and capacity-enhancing investments.

The issue of low-cost firms versus high-cost firms is particularly evident in industries open to foreign competition. Does cost-plus pricing still apply? Are prices in local markets still based on domestic unit production costs? Bloch and Olive (1995) show that the cost-plus approach is generally valid even in open economies. In industries with intense domestic competition, or where foreign competition is weak, foreign companies fix their prices based on the prices set by domestic companies. Foreign companies absorb the losses or rake in the profits associated with changes in exchange rates. In other words, domestic companies remain the price leaders. By contrast, in highly oligopolistic industries with strong potential foreign participation, foreign companies tend to "pass through" the changes in their unit costs and in exchange rates. The cost-plus approach must therefore be modified somewhat, with flexible costing margins taking foreign competition into account.

Also, it should be noted that the profit margin determinants outlined in the preceding section apply under normal conditions. What happens in expansion and in recession when there are fluctuations in demand? Two sets of empirical research offer contradictory evidence. At the aggregate level, researchers find evidence showing that demand fluctuations have an impact on inflation rates that goes beyond their impact on unit labor costs; as a consequence, they conclude that markups are pro-cyclical, moving up when demand is strong, as one would expect based on the standard laws of supply and demand (Atesoglu, 1997; Downward, 1999). On the other hand, at the sectoral level researchers find that real wages are pro-cyclical, rising when demand is strong (Bils, 1985; Barsky *et al.*, 1994). They also find that markups and profit margins are counter-cyclical, moving in an apparently perverse manner. Finally, some studies find no significant relationship between demand fluctuations and the cost margins over normal unit costs (Coutts *et al.*, 1978) or between demand variations and real wages (Kniesser and Goldsmith, 1987). How can these paradoxical sets of findings be reconciled?

Various answers can be advanced. First, aggregate studies may fail to pick up the pro-cyclical pattern of real wages because, in the upswing, the proportion of well-paid overhead labor is likely to fall while less-skilled labor enters the workforce. Since the latter workers earn relatively lower wages, aggregate data would erroneously give the impression that real wages have fallen or that markups have risen (Lavoie, 1996/97). Another possible answer is that the manufacturing sector, the subject of most studies at the microeconomic level, is more unionized than other sectors. Hence, during booms, labor unions in the manufacturing sector manage to obtain large increases in wages relative to labor productivity, thus leading to falling profit margins, something that may not be achieved in other sectors. In the aggregate, it may thus be observed that profit margins rise during the boom and fall during the recession, although the converse occurs in the manufacturing sector. Finally, Chevalier and Scharfstein (1996) provide another explanation of the counter-cyclical movement of profit margins in the manufacturing sector. They argue that firms rely on retained earnings to finance capital accumulation and feel liquidity constrained during recessions; they raise costing margins to relieve these liquidity pressures. During recessions, rates of capacity utilization are lower than normal and target rates of return are not achieved, thus leaving firms strapped for cash in order to fulfill past obligations and finance new investments.

Policy implications and future research

Several important policy implications follow from the Post Keynesian view of pricing. First, the Post Keynesian view of pricing offers an alternative to high unemployment as a means to achieve low inflation rates. Since large corporate firms administer prices anyway, there is no argument against price controls being administered by government authorities. As Galbraith puts in the 1980 introduction of his 1952 book, "it is relatively easy to fix prices that are already fixed."

Second, and this is perhaps the most obvious implication of Post Keynesian pricing theory, prices need not rise during expansions. Where commodities are easily reproducible, more can be produced at a constant unit cost or even at a lower unit cost. In addition, because firms do not necessarily attempt to clear markets, they need not push up costing margins during expansions. The only exception is goods whose production cannot readily be increased, such as raw materials and natural resources. These commodities are often basic goods, required by almost all manufacturing sectors. Raw materials thus constitute the weak point in any expansion, as noted by Kaldor (1976). Both Kaldor and Keynes (1938) proposed new international institutions that would set up buffer stocks and thereby limit fluctuations in world commodity prices. This would help avoid inflationary pressures during expansionary times, and would help governments maintain full-employment policies rather than anti-inflation ones.

To conclude, Post Keynesians rely on a pricing theory with strong links to the real world. Despite the fact that empirical research on pricing has been "stifled by operating within the framework of established theory" (Kaldor, 1985: 54), interviews, surveys, and econometric studies have shown that pricing based on profit maximization and production costs based on diminishing returns are both misguided hypotheses. Rather, firms face approximately constant unit variable costs, and they use cost-plus pricing procedures, often based on some target rate of return.

Future research still needs to ascertain the determinants of these target rates of return over the long haul. In particular, what is the impact of concentration ratios, potential competition, foreign competition, labor unions, productivity growth, secular growth rates in sales, and what is the role of financial variables, such as the rates of interest and debt or liquidity ratios? Field work and econometric research ought to help answer these questions. One reason they have not been provided as yet is that studies on cost margins have been carried out at the level of single products, while the determinants of target rates of return concern the enterprise as a whole[8].

Notes

1 These features of pricing can be found in the work of many authors who have influenced Post Keynesian economics. See Lee (1998) for the historical origins of these various Post Keynesian price theories.

2 In mathematical form, markup pricing is such that: $p = (1 + \theta)\,DC/q$, where p is the price level, θ is the gross cost margin, DC are direct costs, and q is the level of output.

3 The full-cost pricing procedure would yield: $p = (1 + \emptyset)\,TC/q$, where $\emptyset$ is the net costing margin, TC are total costs, and q is the actual level of output.

4 The normal-cost pricing procedure, in its modern version, would yield: $p = (1 + \emptyset)\,TC_s/q_s$, where $\emptyset$ is the net costing margin, TC_s are standard or normal total costs, and q_s is the normal level of output.

5 Target-return pricing procedures use the formula already identified in the case of normal pricing, $p = (1 + \emptyset)\,TC_s/q_s$, but the costing margin is now explicitly defined as: $\emptyset = rv/(u_s - rv)$, where the target rate of return is r, u_s is the standard rate of capacity utilization, and v is the capital-to-capacity ratio. See Lavoie and Ramírez-Gastón (1997) for the application of such a formula within a two-sector model.

6   The main difficulty in this synthesis is that Sraffians define used capital as a joint production process, whereas most Post Keynesians would rather assume the more standard depreciation allowances (depreciation by evaporation).
7   The third component of the target-return pricing formula is the standard rate of capacity utilization.
8   This paper was presented at the 1998 Eastern Economic Association meetings. I am grateful for the comments received there, and also for those made by Harry Bloch, Paul Downward, Ric Holt, John King, Frederic Lee, Steve Pressman, and Mario Seccareccia. I believe these comments have improved the entry substantially. The usual caveats apply.

References

Andrews, P.W.S. (1949) *Manufacturing Business*, London: Macmillan.

Andrews, P.W.S. and Brunner, E. (1975) *Studies in Pricing*, London: Macmillan.

Atesoglu, H.S. (1997) "A Post Keynesian Explanation of U.S. Inflation," *Journal of Post Keynesian Economics*, 19: 639–49.

Barsky, R., Solon, G. and Parker, J. (1994) "Measuring the Cyclicality of Real Wages: How Important is Composition Bias?" *Quarterly Journal of Economics*, 109,1: 1–26.

Bhaduri, A. (1986) *Macro-Economics: The Dynamics of Commodity Production*, Armonk, NY: M.E. Sharpe.

Bils, M. (1985) "Real Wages Over The Business Cycle: Evidence From Panel Data," *Journal of Political Economy*, 93: 666–89.

Bloch, H. and Olive, M. (1995) "Can Simple Rules Explain Pricing Behavior in Australian Manufacturing," *Australian Economic Papers*, 35: 1–19.

Boggio, L. (1992) "Production Prices and Dynamic Stability: Results and Open Questions," *Manchester School*, 60(3): 264–94.

Brunner, E. (1952) "Competition and the Theory of the Firm: Part II – Price Determination and the Working of Competition," *Economia Internazionale*, 5(4): 727–44.

Capoglu, G. (1991) *Prices, Profits and Financial Structures: A Post-Keynesian Approach to Competition*, Aldershot: Edward Elgar.

Chevalier, J.A. and Scharfstein, D.S. (1996) "Capital-market Imperfections and Countercyclical Markups: Theory and Evidence," *American Economic Review*, 86: 703–25.

Coutts, K., Godley, W. and Nordhaus, W. (1978) *Industrial Pricing in the United Kingdom*, Cambridge: Cambridge University Press.

Cowling, K. (1982) *Monopoly Capitalism*, London: Macmillan.

Downward, P. (1999) *Pricing Theory in Post Keynesian Economics: A Realist Approach*, Cheltenham: Edward Elgar.

Eichner, A.S. (1987) *The Macrodynamics of Advanced Market Economies*, Armonk, NY: M.E. Sharpe.

Galbraith, J.K. (1952) *A Theory of Price Control*, Cambridge: Cambridge University Press.

Hall, R.L. and Hitch, C.L. (1939) "Price Theory and Business Behavior," *Oxford Economic Papers*, 1(2): 12–45.

Harcourt, G. and Kenyon, P. (1976) "Pricing and the Investment Decision," *Kyklos*, 29: 449–77.

Harrod, R.F. (1973) *Economic Dynamics*, London: Macmillan.

Kaldor, N. (1976) "Inflation and Recession in the World Economy," *Economic Journal*, 86: 703–14.

Kaldor, N. (1982) *The Scourge of Monetarism*, Oxford: Oxford University Press.

Kaldor, N. (1985) *Economics without Equilibrium*, Armonk, NY: M.E. Sharpe.

Kalecki, M. (1971) *Selected Essays on the Dynamics of the Capitalist Economy*, Cambridge: Cambridge University Press.

Kaplan, A.D.H., Dirlam, J.B. and Lanzillotti, R.F. (1958) *Pricing in Big Business: A Case Approach*, Washington, DC: Brookings Institution.

Keynes, J.M. [1938] (1983) "The Policy of Government Storage of Foodstuffs and Raw Materials," in *The Collected Writings of John Maynard Keynes*, vol. XXI, London: Macmillan, pp. 456–70.

Kniesser, T.J. and Goldsmith, A.H. (1987) "A Survey of Alternative Models of the Aggregate US Labor Market," *Journal of Economic Literature*, 25: 1241–80.

Koutsoyiannis, A. (1984) "Goals of oligopolistic firms," *Southern Economic Journal*, 51: 540–567.

Lanzillotti, R.F. (1958) "Pricing Objectives in Large Companies," *American Economic Review*, 48: 921–40.

Lavoie, M. (1992) *Foundations of Post-Keynesian Economic Analysis*, Aldershot: Edward Elgar.

Lavoie, M. (1996) "Unproductive Outlays and Capital Accumulation with Target-return Pricing," *Review of Social Economy*, 54(3): 303–321.

Lavoie, M. (1996/97) "Real Wages, Employment Structure, and the Aggregate Demand Curve in a Kaleckian Short Run Model," *Journal of Post Keynesian Economics*, 19(2): 275–88.

Lavoie, M. and Ramírez-Gastón, P. (1997) "Traverse in a Two-sector Kaleckian Model of Growth with Target Return Pricing," *Manchester School of Economic and Social Studies*, 55(1): 145–169.

Lee, F.S. (1985) "Full Cost Prices, Classical Price Theory, and Long Period Method Analysis: a Critical Evaluation," *Metroeconomica*, 37(2): 199–219.

Lee, F.S. (1994) "From Post-Keynesian to Historical Price Theory. Part 1: Facts, Theory and Empirically Grounded Pricing Model," *Review of Political Economy*, 6(3): 303–36.

Lee, F.S. (1998) *Post Keynesian Price Theory*, Cambridge: Cambridge University Press.

Lee, F.S., Irving-Lessman, J., Earl, P. and Davies, J.E. (1986), "P.W.S. Andrews' Theory of Competitive Oligopoly: A New Interpretation," *British Review of Economic Issues*, 8: 13–39.

Nell, E. (1988) *Prosperity and Public Spending: Transformational Growth and the Role of Government*, Boston: Unwin Hyman.

Pivetti, M. (1985) "On the Monetary Explanation of Distribution, *Political Economy*, 1(2): 73–103.

Robinson, J. (1977) "Michal Kalecki on the economics of capitalism," *Oxford Bulletin of Economics and Statistics*, 39 (1), 7–17.

Rowthorn, R.E. (1981) "Demand, Real Wages and Economic Growth," *Thames Papers in Political Economy*, Autumn: 1–39.

Shipley, D.D. (1981) "Pricing Objectives in British Manufacturing Industry," *Journal of Industrial Economics*, 29(4): 429–443.

Steindl, J. (1952) *Maturity and Stagnation in American Capitalism*, Oxford: Basil Blackwell.

Sylos Labini, P. (1962) *Oligopoly and Technical Progress*, Cambridge: Harvard University Press.

Wood, A. (1975) *A Theory of Profits*, Cambridge: Cambridge University Press.

4   The distribution of income

James K. Galbraith

Introduction

Michael Lind has called income inequality "the prevailing social issue of our time." These days, the designation meets little argument.[1] But this development is recent. Income inequality in postwar America began to rise only in 1970, and the re-emergence of inequality as a social issue dates only to the late 1980s. It took Reaganism to reawaken class consciousness in American political life. Before that, attention had been on other issues.

The original submergence of class was a liberal achievement. Perhaps John Maynard Keynes's greatest service to capitalism is that he focused attention on jobs; unemployment and not equality was the great issue of the Great Depression. And in the Keynesian period from 1945 to 1970 income inequality received scant scholarly attention. The great income leveling achieved during World War II shifted attention to poverty as the organizing principle for social action.[2]

And so the theory of income distribution passed into the domain of microeconomics. Textbooks taught neoclassical marginal productivity theory, loosely rooted in two-factor production functions. On this view, profits are the just reward of capital and wages are proportional to personal productivities, duly adjusted by stocks of human capital. The theory nicely explained the stability of income shares between profits and wages as reflecting the slowly changing and neutral character of technological change.[3] The theory also predicted a smooth relationship between the rate of interest and the capital intensity of technique. As interest rates declined, profit maximization would dictate an evolution toward greater capital intensity and lower marginal productivity of the capital stock.

This is the context for the uprising that became known as "the Cambridge Capital Critique" (see Harcourt, 1973), which began in the 1950s with the observation by Joan Robinson (1956) that there were difficulties in assuming a unit of measure for the capital stock.

Brief statement of the starting position

Jan Kregel's (1978) essay on "Income distribution" in the first *Guide to Post Keynesian Economics* remains a classic introduction to the work of Kalecki,

Robinson, Kaldor, Sraffa, Pasinetti, Harcourt, and others on this issue. I can scarcely improve on that work. This chapter will therefore focus on developments since 1978, and on what I believe to be the most promising way forward for future research. Still, it is useful to begin with a brief review of the original controversy, and what it means for the micro-theoretic view of income distribution.

In the 1950s and 1960 Joan Robinson and Piero Sraffa raised serious objections to the neoclassical proposition that the distribution of factor income could logically be interpreted as a set of factor returns related to marginal productivities under constant returns to scale. Robinson presented the "special theory" of this critique, namely that the concept of aggregate capital as a physical quantity was incoherent. Capital goods cannot be aggregated into a common measure of "the capital stock" without first assigning a value to each physical capital item. But treating the capital stock as a value aggregate requires prior knowledge of the rate of interest. The value of a particular capital good depends on the future net revenue stream attributable to the acquisition of that good, discounted at a rate of interest; capital goods will be acquired up to the point where their internal rate of return (marginal efficiency) just equals that rate of interest. How can the neoclassical rate of interest then be the marginal productivity of capital that the theory was supposed to determine? Robinson identified a logical inconsistency at the heart of neoclassical distribution theory. Furthermore, under simple alternative specifications that admitted the heterogeneity of capital goods, the smooth inverse relationship between interest rates and capital intensity would not hold. This was re-switching.

Sraffa's contribution was to generalize the argument of Robinson and render the concept of marginal productivity redundant. Sraffa (1960) showed that short-period production prices can be derived from dated physical quantities of embodied labor input (and an exogenous discount or interest rate), as Marx had postulated but without satisfactory proof. Relative prices, and for that matter relative wages, therefore do not depend on marginal productivities. Meanwhile, Keynes supplied a theory of the interest rate built on liquidity preference, and so eliminated the need for a marginal physical productivity of the aggregate capital stock to underpin the theory of the rate of interest.

It followed that aggregate income distribution, the division of national product between wages and profits, must be determined by some mechanism other than the marginal rate of return on an alleged capital stock. But what mechanism?

Keynes, Kalecki (1971) and Kaldor presented the Post Keynesian position on this question – "capitalists get what they spend." Aggregate profits are determined by the spending decisions of the capitalist class. Business people, motivated by animal spirits, receive back as profit income what they spend as capital investment and luxury consumption. Aggregate wages, on the other hand, get determined by the aggregate stock of consumption goods produced; they are a function of effective demand for output. Average wages are just aggregate wages divided by the total number of workers.

If workers save, as Pasinetti (1974) showed, the flow of profit income runs partly to workers. But, other things equal, the aggregate volume of profit income is unaffected. In other words, total profits depend entirely on business and government spending decisions, and not on the distribution of claims to profit income. Nor do they depend on the quality or type of spending. Finally, the personal distribution of wage income gets left entirely up in the air – to be settled by political, institutional, and historical forces.

The ratio between aggregate wages and gross profits is the national distribution of income. After a slump, exhilaration takes over and investment soars. An investment-and-profits boom leads back to full employment. In times of full employment, with consumption and wages high, there is a profits squeeze and business gets "boom-tired." Artificial booms are possible. For example, the government can provide a stimulus to spending if private businesses are unwilling to do so; but such initiatives are met with ambivalence by business leaders since they deprive them of their controlling position in the political economy.

The argument since 1978

The critique of Robinson and Sraffa is more than forty years old. Yet for psychological and political reasons, rather than for logical and mathematical ones, the capital critique has not penetrated mainstream economics. It likely never will. Today only a handful of economists seem aware of it. Aggregate production function applications run rampant in studies of economic growth (new growth theory), development and convergence, and international trade (factor-price equalization and other applications of Heckscher–Ohlin). Ostensible liberals are not exempt; their arguments for higher public infrastructure investment (based on its alleged marginal productivity) are precisely of this type, as are arguments for increased investment in education based on the higher marginal productivity of human skill.[4] To mainstream economics, Keynesianism has been reduced to a narrow doctrine relating sticky wages, public spending, and employment. The fact that there exists a Post Keynesian distribution theory, still less the reasons for it, has been mostly forgotten.

Thus, when inequality resurfaced as a social and political economic issue in the 1980s, economists responded with a flood of new studies founded in microeconomics. It is perhaps a mark of the capital controversies that these rarely, if ever, refer to non-labor income, nor attempt to rationalize the vast rise of profits in the early 1990s as a response to the "rising marginal productivity of capital." The debate over increasing inequality has been conducted almost exclusively in pre-Sraffian and anti-Keynesian terms; that is, in terms of the pricing of underlying factors of production and their marginal productivities. The idiom is competitive supply-and-demand models operating under conditions of diminishing marginal returns.

The point of contention in these inequality debates has been over the timeless issue of demand versus supply. Is rising inequality due to an increase in the relative demand for (read, a rise in the marginal physical productivity of) highly skilled workers (Bound and Johnson, 1992)? Or is it due to an increase in the supply of low-skill workers, through immigration (Borjas and Ramey, 1994)? Or is trade (Wood, 1994) driving down the marginal wage (along a fixed marginal productivity schedule)? In all cases, the argument respects the marginal productivity paradigm and the market mechanism.

The empirical literature on this topic is interesting. Juhn *et al.* (1993) show how rising inequality in the US during the 1970s was mainly due to the falling position of the bottom half of the wage distribution; it is only in the 1980s that the top half also spreads out, with a corresponding increase in the estimated value of years of schooling. Krueger (1993) shows how higher wage differentials are associated with the use of computers at the workplace, though as Lawrence (1997), Krueger (1993), and others now acknowledge, the direction of causation in this relationship is far from certain. Carnoy (1995), Howell and Gittleman (1993), and others have noted that skill differentials and wage differentials do not always move together: for African-Americans, the former have narrowed but the latter have increased. Thurow (1998), citing a study by Houseman (1995), points out that while the wage gap between high school and college graduates increased, real wages in both groups declined. What sort of technological progress is this?

In practice, mainstream analysts downplay supply factors and emphasize the skill bias in technological change. Yet the impression left by surveys (Danziger and Gottschalk, 1996; Lawrence, 1997) is that of evidentiary impasse, with the final result dominated by the assumptions of conventional thinking. It may be that the core empirical issues will never be resolved to the entire satisfaction of the contestants. It is even less likely that this work will provide a satisfactory examination of the underlying theoretical questions.

At the same time, the literature is vulnerable to a Post Keynesian critique. To make such a critique persuasive requires a clear theoretical restatement, going beyond the usual appeal to institutions, politics, and history. But it also requires a persuasive empirical substantiation, one capable of accounting for the movement of inequality through time and in different national settings. Post Keynesians need to show that the personal distribution of income is linked to the flow of economic profits as a share of national income, and therefore to the spending decisions of capitalists and their macroeconomic ramifications. They need to show this, not only for the US, but for a wide range of countries. The Post Keynesian theory of income distribution is not specific to the US.

For this we need more and better data, particularly better measures of economic inequality through time, so that the relationship between inequality and macroeconomic phenomena can be tracked. A macroeconomic theory of distribution requires macroeconomic measures of distribution. Fortunately, this condition can be met. The requisite information is available in the historical record, over long time spans and for many countries. Until recently, however, its potential for this purpose has rarely been recognized and almost never exploited (see Galbraith and Berner, 2001).

Toward a macroeconomic theory of personal income distribution

Consider a simple setting: an economy with one production factor (labor), and firms with identical rising marginal production costs, but distinct markets. One firm faces a competitive, perfectly elastic demand curve and prices at marginal cost. Another firm faces a downward-sloping demand curve and sets output so that marginal revenue equals marginal cost, with price taken from the corresponding point on the demand function [as first stipulated by Joan Robinson (1933)]. The second firm enjoys a degree of monopoly equal to the inverse of the elasticity of the demand function, per Abba Lerner (1934), and a monopoly return per unit equal to the difference between price and marginal cost. Since this model has no capital, there is no profit either. The monopoly return must be distributed to the sole factor of production, namely labor: it is a firm-specific labor rent. The distribution of income therefore depends entirely on the relative degree of monopoly power.

This is the simple theory of personal income distribution that follows from the Post Keynesian view of pricing (see Chapter 3). Sraffa's pricing scheme, although worked out for the competitive setting, does not exclude monopoly power. Rather, it rules out the notion of a separate return to capital, and therefore a coherent idea of profit as a factor return. Rent and quasi-rent, on the other hand, remain viable. And there is no reason why certain classes of labor cannot earn scarcity premia, just as certain grades of land do. The premium commanded by the purveyor of a new machine, so often referred to as a return to capital or to technological innovation, is simply the scarcity rent commanded by the labor that produced it. Remove the patent protection or veil of secrecy surrounding the technique embodied in the machine and the return will collapse, even though marginal productivity in a technical sense is unaffected.

Now consider the effect of an equal and proportionate upward shift in the demand function facing the two firms. In the competitive case, prices (and wage rates, which by assumption make up marginal cost) rise along the marginal cost function. But in the monopolistic case, the slope of the marginal revenue function assures that price will not rise to the full extent of the shift in demand. Furthermore, since the wage rate in the monopolistic case already includes a substantial element of quasi-rent, the proportionate shift in the wage must be lower, given the identical shift in the demand function. For these reasons, an outward shift in demand will raise the wage of the competitive sector relative to that of the monopolistic sector, reducing the difference between the two and therefore the degree of inequality in the system as a whole. An inward shift will have the opposite effect.

Two results emerge from this analysis. First, because of rent-sharing, firms facing less elastic demand functions should pay higher wages than firms facing more elastic demand functions. Second, the degree of dispersion in the wage structure should vary with macroeconomic conditions: it should fall during booms and rise during slumps. In other words, most countries should be found on the downward-sloping portion of an inverted Kuznets U curve; economic growth should equalize incomes and recession should increase inequality. These predictions differ from the neoclassical view, which holds that monopoly rents flow to capitalists (rather than to workers) and which sees no connection between the microeconomically determined personal distribution of wages and the business cycle.

This is a good beginning, but it is not quite enough. One needs a rationale for the existence of monopoly power and downward-sloping demand curves facing firms. This is to be found in the existence of machines, which embody past labor frozen for current and future use. It is the machinery used in production, and nothing else, that permits one final product to be distinguished from another and that makes possible the differentiation of individual firm demand curves. Once title to machinery is vested in the capitalist, some of the monopoly rent may be paid to that person. But this does not undermine our conclusion, since the salary paid to an owner-executive is not distinguishable from employee wages in accounting terms. And a larger portion of the monopoly rent also flows downward through the salary and wage structure, reaching managers and even production workers in the form of efficiency wages. Everyone connected with machinery benefits and has an advantage over those not so connected.

Our two firms can be reinterpreted as representing two sectors in the economy. One sector works entirely with current labor, supplied competitively, and prices output at a conventional but small mark-up over a socially determined minimum wage. We might call this the S sector; it resembles the largest parts of the services sector in real life. The other sector we may call the C sector. It produces ordinary machinery and consumption goods from current labor and existing machines, which is to say from current labor plus a potpourri of embodied past labor over which the firm holds ownership rights. Since each potpourri is in some respects unique, the essence of monopoly power is right there; it lies in the particularity of manufactured output and the corresponding differentiation of consumer demand.[5]

The still-missing element is a central one in capitalist economic life, the defining characteristic of advanced industrial countries. It is the creation and production of new products, machinery, and means of production. This is, in large part, the function of a separate, specialized sector which we may call the K sector – producers of knowledge goods.

From the standpoint of distribution theory, the income of the K sector corresponds to the Keynes–Kalecki–Kaldor flow of profits. It is determined by capitalist spending. Since capitalists purchase investment goods, a swing in the flow of gross investment corresponds to an income swing in the K sector. The Keynes–Kalecki proposition that capitalist consumption (expenditure on non-wage goods) also enhances the flow of profits has its material counterpart in the observation that non-wage goods, or luxury consumption, are merely advanced-technology investment goods adapted for personal enjoyment. In a cyclical economy, the K sector will be a strongly cyclical performer. The cycle itself is above all a cycle of capitalist spending.

Production in the K sector is not based primarily on the accumulation of past labor inputs, organized as a specific stock of machines, but rather on the accumulation of people and their skills. Like the C sector, the K sector is monopolistic, but in an unstable way. Monopoly power in this sector is inherently transient, and depends on fabricating new markets and extracting maximal revenue from these markets while they last. The K sector is Schumpeterian. It is the sphere of creative destruction, a winner-take-all proposition, a lottery, in which the game of competition is to beat the competition with new products and better processes. Wages in the K sector are necessarily high, both because the prizes are great and because there is nothing to be gained from second-rate talent.

On the other hand, employment in the K sector is radically dependent on the flow of investment demand. The K sector is the central producer of new capital equipment. Its prosperity depends on a high rate of acquiring such equipment. Correspondingly, it also depends on a high rate of destruction for old capital equipment. The K sector therefore benefits, as the C sector does not, from a strong cycle in investment spending, both from the downturn that wipes out the old and obsolescent and again from the upturn when new plants and processes move into the vacuum left by the old.

In advanced industrial countries, a rise in business investment at the start of expansions increases employment among high wage groups, such as construction and technology workers, and especially among their non-production workers – the designers, marketers, managers, etc. At first, high rates of growth increase both inequality and the average real wage. Only as the expansion proceeds, as higher incomes are paid to production workers and as demand shifts to consumer products and services, will the income-compressing effects of prosperity be felt. In short, investment demand is unequalizing, whereas consumption demand is equalizing.

Extending this analysis to the foreign sector is simple. In an advanced economy, such as the US, K-sector goods dominate exports and C-sector goods dominate the competition with imports. Since the K sector is hypermonopolistic, it has few developing-country competitors. Changes in the (north–south) exchange rate do not greatly affect it. But such changes do undercut the relative wages of C-sector workers by adjusting, in effect, the relative wages of their direct competition. Since K-sector workers sit at the top of the wage structure, currency appreciations tend to increase inequality in advanced countries and currency depreciations to decrease it. Also, export booms in an advanced country tend to raise inequality in the wage structure, as do the corresponding increases in imports. In countries lacking a K sector, investment demand leaks to imports, and economic growth is equalizing in so far as the domestic economy is concerned.

We thus have a macroeconomic theory of the evolution of the personal income distribution, according to which inequality varies with the movements of aggregate demand, differentiated by sector. In advanced countries, investment booms increase inequality, consumption booms decrease it, and the exchange rate plus patterns of foreign demand govern the patterns of effect from the foreign sector.[6]

Evidence on the macro-theory of income distribution

To evaluate a macroeconomic theory of personal income distribution one needs dense time series information on the evolution of inequality in many countries. Unfortunately, few nations have consistent annual household surveys from which inequality measures can be computed over long time horizons. Existing survey results tend to focus on income by family or household, measures that can be quite far removed from the structure of hourly wage rates by industry and occupation. Industrial data in household surveys can be sketchy and, in contrast to information on age or gender or ethnicity, such data are subject to high rates of error in reporting.

But there is an alternative approach to measuring the changing dispersion of hourly wage rates, particularly if one is principally interested in the manufacturing sector. This is the generalized entropy approach of Theil (1972), based on information theory. Theil's measure has the virtue that changes in inequality can be estimated from very crude data on wages or earnings and employment grouped by industrial sector. Industrial data sets, organized into standard classification schemes, are available on a consistent annual basis for most countries in the world. They provide a rich, and so far largely unexplored, source from which estimates of the movement of industrial wage inequality through time can be computed.

Empirical work using this approach suggests that in virtually every industrializing country there is a negative association between growth and inequality. Rapid growth is equalizing; most countries are on the downward-sloping portion of the Kuznets inverted U curve. Among significant exceptions are the US and the UK. In these cases, we find a strong positive association between unemployment and inequality. But after controlling for the effects of unemployment, inflation, and the exchange rate (all of which have signs predicted by the macroeconomic theory), growth increases inequality to a modest degree. This would appear to reflect the influence of the cycle of profit spending on employment and incomes in the K sector – just as predicted (see Galbraith, 1998; Galbraith and Berner, 2001).

Summary and conclusions

Post Keynesians challenged the marginal productivity theory of distribution long ago. They also presented the outlines of an alternative theory, whose major elements are the distribution of labor rents, affected by differing degrees of monopoly power, and the flow of profit spending and therefore of investment, which corresponds to the income of the sector producing investment goods, and especially technology goods. But the Post Keynesians did not succeed. What they lacked was a demonstration of the superiority of this theory as the foundation for empirical research into the functional and personal distributions of income. In consequence, neoclassical theory has continued to shape the literature.

Today, advances in the measurement of inequality, coupled with careful attention to issues of taxonomy in the industrial structure, permit a demonstration that major movements in the inequality of wage structures are traceable to macroeconomic events. They closely correspond to performance patterns of the major Keynesian sectors: investment, consumption, foreign trade. One may hope that the combination of theory and evidence can change some minds about which theory of income distribution is appropriate to the modern world. Perhaps this approach may enjoy more success than the purely logical critiques of the mid twentieth century.[7]

Notes

1 "It Takes A Nation," *The Washington Monthly*, November 1998.
2 In the 1950s, John Kenneth Galbraith (1958: 82) observed that "few things are more evident in modern social history than the decline of interest in inequality as an economic issue." Michael Harrington's (1962) *The Other America* is widely credited with mobilizing interest in poverty. In the context of a world that saw itself as prosperous, egalitarian, and fully employed, the poor were "other." Poverty became defined as separation from the capitalist system rather than as an extension of it.
3 It also provided an irrefutable and empty rationalization for existing wage differentials since human capital cannot, by its nature, be observed or measured to any useful degree of precision.
4 Aggregation of human capital (heterogeneous education acquired at different moments in past time) faces exactly the same problems as aggregation of physical capital. The (needless to say, ludicrous) response of the literature is to treat all moments in school as identical and timeless, so that they can be added and compared, once and for all, for each worker.
5 There is, of course, a certain amount of monopoly rent in human talent, the "winner-take-all" phenomenon of sports stars and divas admirably dealt with by Cook and Frank (1996). But compared with product differentiation this phenomenon is minor.
6 To this, one might add a fourth source of differentiated aggregate demand, namely that from the military sector, whose effect will depend specifically on the composition of military spending. Typically, the military sector combines an emphasis on advanced technologies with high wage rates among production workers.
7 This essay is a project of the University of Texas Inequality Project, and was prepared with support from the Levy Institute and the Ford Foundation. It has appeared in slightly altered form as Chapter one of Galbraith and Berner (2001), published by Cambridge University Press and used here with permission. Comments are welcome and may be directed to Galbraith@mail.utexas.edu. I thank Steve Pressman, and especially Paul Davidson, for exceptionally detailed and useful comments.

References

Borjas, G.J. and Ramey, V.A. (1994) "The Relationship Between Wage Inequality and International Trade," in J.H. Bergstrand *et al.* (eds.) *The Changing Distribution of Income in an Open U.S. Economy*, Amsterdam: Elsevier, pp. 215–41.

Bound, J. and Johnson, G. (1992) "Changes in the Structure of Wages in the 1980s: An Evaluation of Alternative Explanations," *American Economic Review*, 82: 371–92.

Carnoy, M. (1995) *Faded Dreams: The Politics and Economics of Race in America*, Cambridge: Cambridge University Press.

Cook, P. and Frank, R. (1996) *The Winner-Take-All Society*, New York: The Free Press.

Danziger, S. and Gottschalk, P. (1996) *America Unequal*, Cambridge: Harvard University Press.

Galbraith, J.K. (1998) *Created Unequal: The Crisis in American Pay*, New York: Free Press.

Galbraith, J.K. and Berner, M. (2001) *Inequality and Industrial Change: A Global View*, New York: Cambridge University Press.

Galbraith, John K. (1958) *The Affluent Society*, Boston: Houghton Mifflin.

Harcourt, G. (1973) *Some Cambridge Controversies in the Theory of Capital*, Cambridge: Cambridge University Press.

Harrington, M. (1962) *The Other America: Poverty in the United States*, New York: Macmillan.

Houseman, S. (1995) "Job Growth and the Quality of Jobs in the US Economy," W.E. Upjohn Institute, Staff Working Papers.

Howell, D.R. and Gittleman, M.B. (1993) "Job, Labor Market Segmentation in the 1980's: A New Perspective on the Effects of Employment Restructuring by Race and Gender," New School for Social Research, mimeo.

Juhn, C., Murphy, K. and Pierce, B. (1993) "Wage Inequality and the Rise in Returns to Skill," *Journal of Political Economy*, 101: 410–42.

Kalecki, M. (1971) "The Determinants of Profits," in *Selected Essays in the Dynamics of the Capitalist Economy*, Cambridge: Cambridge University Press, pp. 78–92.

Kregel, J. (1978) "Income Distribution," in A. Eichner (ed.) *A Guide to Post-Keynesian Economics*, Armonk: M.E. Sharpe, pp. 46–60.

Krueger, A. (1993) "How Computers have changed the Wage Structure: Evidence from Microdata, 1984–1989," *Quarterly Journal of Economics*, 108: 33–60.

Lawrence, R.Z. (1997) *Single World, Divided Nations?* Washington: Brookings Institution and OECD Development Center.

Lerner, A.P. (1934) "The Concept of Monopoly and the Measurement of Monopoly Power," *Review of Economic Studies*, 1: 157–75.

Pasinetti, L. (1974) *Growth and Income Distribution: Essays in Economic Theory*, London: Cambridge University Press.

Robinson, J. (1933) *The Economics of Imperfect Competition*, London: Macmillan.

Robinson, J. (1956) *The Accumulation of Capital*, London: Macmillan.

Sraffa, P. (1960) *Production of Commodities by Means of Commodities*, Cambridge: Cambridge University Press.

Theil, H. (1972) *Statistical Decomposition Analysis: With Applications in the Social and Administrative Sciences*, Amsterdam: North Holland.

Thurow, L. (1998) "Wage dispersion: 'Who Done it?'" *Journal of Post Keynesian Economics*, 21(1): 25–37.

Wood, A. (1994) *North–South Trade, Employment and Inequality*, Oxford: Clarendon Press.

5　Tax incidence

Anthony J. Laramie and Douglas Mair

Introduction

Tax incidence examines who bears the burden of taxation. Economists who study this subject distinguish legal tax incidence from economic tax incidence. Legal tax incidence refers to who is legally liable to make tax payments to the government. Economic tax incidence studies how after-tax incomes are affected by a tax.

Tax incidence is typically one of the first applications of supply and demand analysis presented to economics students. The application contradicts common perceptions that consumers bear the full burden of a sales tax or an excise tax, and reveals the great power of economic reasoning. Students learn that market demand will not bear a price increase equal to the tax increase. As a result, both consumers (through an increase in market price) and producers (through a reduction in after-tax profits) will pay part of the tax. Students then come to realize that the shares of the tax burden depend on the price elasticities of demand and supply, *ceteris paribus*. Students also realize that economic tools can reveal unseen forces and generate counter-intuitive conclusions. For these reasons economists have had a long-standing fascination with tax incidence.

Two leading neoclassical public finance economists, Kotlikoff and Summers (1987: 1088), contend that incidence theory is fun as well as informative because it provides a rich assortment of insights that contradict initial impressions. It is also important because of its implications for the impact of government policies. But Kotlikoff and Summers admit that much of the tax incidence literature assumes certainty, perfect information and market clearing. They also recognize that more sophisticated models are required to relax these assumptions, and that such models should yield even more surprising and exciting economic insights. The Post Keynesian theory of tax incidence does just this – it relaxes the core assumptions of the neoclassical theory in order to generate important conclusions and insights.

As suggested above, the microeconomic analysis of tax incidence in a partial equilibrium world where demand and supply schedules are known is quite straightforward. But when tax feedback effects are present, or where taxes affect the distribution of income (and thus aggregate demand and economic growth), the theory of tax incidence becomes quite complicated.

Orthodox theory takes a microeconomic approach to understanding tax incidence. The incidence of a tax is revealed in the tax wedge between the pre-tax price and the after-tax price or between pre-tax income and after-tax income. Introducing a tax alters relative prices and introduces substitution effects. The strength of these substitution effects determines the incidence of a tax. At the macroeconomic level (where microeconomic foundations are assumed to operate), aggregate income and employment are constrained (by assumption) at full employment by supply-side factors. The incidence of a tax is again analyzed in the context of changing relative prices and substitution effects.

In the Post Keynesian tradition, both microeconomic and macroeconomic foundations exist. Microeconomic decisions about pricing and the markup (see Chapter 3) influence the distribution of income. The impact of taxation on the cost–markup relationship influences the distribution of income. The distribution of income, in turn, influences aggregate demand. Aggregate demand then influences aggregate production, incomes, and employment.

At the macroeconomic level, the overall performance of the economy is determined by spending flows. Taxation can affect aggregate spending in a number of ways within this framework. Taxation affects the government budget, consumption out of profits and wages, net exports, and business investment. The extent to which taxation affects overall spending determines the impact of taxation on aggregate incomes, and thereby the behavior of individual economic agents. From a Post Keynesian perspective both the microeconomic and macroeconomic effects of taxation must be considered together in assessing the incidence of taxation.

The main distinction between the Post Keynesian approach and the orthodox approach is that the former allows demand-side constraints, treats aggregate income as a variable (allows it to change), and recognizes that cost markups are determined in imperfectly competitive markets. In both the orthodox and Post Keynesian approaches, the theory of tax incidence is applied to income distribution theory. In the orthodox approach, the study of income distribution is based upon marginal productivity theory. In the Post Keynesian approach, aggregate demand and market power together determine the distribution of income.

Post Keynesian tax incidence theory stems from Kalecki (1937). Before we consider the Post Keynesian theory in more detail, we first consider the orthodox approach to tax incidence.

The orthodox theory of tax incidence

A. (Tom) Asimakopulos (1978) wrote the chapter on tax incidence in the first Post Keynesian *Guide*. Asimakopulos, with Burbidge (1974), developed Kalecki's theory of tax incidence. Their work explicitly considered the difficulties with the orthodox approach to tax incidence. Leading neoclassical economists working in this area (Atkinson and Stiglitz, 1980; Kotlikoff and Summers,

1987; Stern, 1992; Musgrave, 1997) also think that the orthodox approach has problems and that neoclassical theory has proceeded down a blind alley.

The problems with the orthodox approach stem from the assumptions that define its theoretical core. The assumptions of market clearing, perfect competition, full employment (and no aggregate demand effects), perfect certainty (or its counterpart rational expectations), and the marginal productivity theory of production and income distribution all fail to reflect some the essential features of real world economies. For example, the marginal productivity theory of income distribution is inappropriate because it requires continual full employment. In addition, Burbidge (1976) showed that many empirical neoclassical studies of the incidence of the corporation tax were inconsistent because their microeconomic foundations were pre-Keynesian, on which they then grafted *ad hoc* cyclical variables whose very existence was denied by the microeconomic theory. Many years later this problem still bedevils neoclassical tax incidence theory.

In the late twentieth century, the neoclassical approach became preoccupied with optimal taxation. However laudable its efforts in trying to minimize the welfare costs of taxes, the neoclassical approach does not address what Post Keynesians perceive to be the more important issue – the dynamic effects of taxation. Consequently, neoclassical theory finds itself in an impasse. As Stern (1992: 273) writes, "The theory of optimal taxation has not had a great deal to say about dynamics and the theory of growth has been reticent on taxation."

A big advance in the neoclassical theory of tax incidence occurred with the publication of an influential paper by Harberger (1962). Using a two-sector, two-factor model borrowed from international trade theory (and making all the conventional neoclassical assumptions of profit maximizing, perfect competition, perfect factor mobility, etc.), Harberger showed that a profits tax must fall on the earnings of firms because they have no scope, by assumption, to increase pre-tax profits. The Harberger model spawned a rash of studies in the 1960s and 1970s on the incidence of the corporation income tax but, as we have noted above, Burbidge (1976) demonstrated that they are all flawed.

Undeterred, neoclassical economists have continued to study the effects of corporate taxation on investment while ignoring tax incidence questions. They typically express the rate of investment as a function of the shadow price of capital (the discounted sum of "spot" marginal revenue products over the life of the capital good evaluated at the time of the investment decision) minus the relative price of capital, adjusted for taxes, taking into account the adjustment costs associated with capital investment and expectations based on the information available to the firm at the time of the investment decision.

Within this general family of neoclassical models, the Brainard and Tobin (1968) Q model has been employed extensively. The intuition underlying Q models derives from Keynes (1936: 151):

> [D]aily revaluations of the Stock Exchange ... exert a decisive influence on the rate of current investment. For there is no sense in building up a

new enterprise at a cost greater than that at which a similar existing enterprise can be purchased; whilst there is an inducement to spend on a new project what may seem an extravagant sum, if it can be floated off on the Stock Exchange at an immediate profit.

This intuition has been formalized to demonstrate the existence of a relationship between investment and Marginal Q, the ratio of the discounted future revenues from an additional unit of capital to its purchase price. Because Marginal Q is unobservable, neoclassical researchers have used observable Average Q, which they legitimize by assuming that:

1   product and factor markets are competitive;.
2   production and adjustment cost technologies are linear homogeneous;
3   capital is homogeneous; and
4   investment decisions are largely separate from other real and financial decisions.

It is obvious that this approach perpetuates the theoretical inconsistency between the microeconomic and macroeconomic elements of neoclassical models that we have referred to above. Post Keynesian economists find it difficult to accept Chirinko's (1993) claim that dynamic Q-type models are theoretically consistent.

These neoclassical models do less well empirically. Chirinko (1993) finds that dynamic neoclassical models examining the effects of taxation on investment have mixed performance results. They generally fail to produce high R^2 values and they fail specification tests. Q models have performed particularly poorly (Blundell *et al.*, 1992).

The Post Keynesian approach

Post Keynesian tax incidence theory was inspired by Kalecki. Kalecki recognized that Keynes's theory of effective demand required a whole new approach to taxation; and it was Keynes, as editor of the *Economic Journal*, who published Kalecki's important 1937 paper on tax incidence.

Kalecki, having recognized the need for a new approach to the theory of taxation, unfortunately did not develop a fully worked out theory. He did set out the bare bones of a theory explaining how the taxation of commodities, income, and capital would affect the level of aggregate demand, but only within the framework of a short-period model. While this was undoubtedly a major advance in the theory of taxation, Kalecki never returned to this theme in his subsequent writings. Most of his later work on investment and business cycles expressly assumed away any role for taxation and government activity.

Having developed a theory of effective demand and a macroeconomic theory of income distribution early in the 1930s, Kalecki then moved on to look at tax incidence. His theory was developed from his now famous profit function derived from the national accounts. On the income side, national income equals wages plus profits. On the expenditure side, national income equals consumption out of wages plus consumption out of profits plus investment plus government expenditures. So, gross (pre-tax) profits equals investment + government purchases – wage taxes + consumption out of profits – worker savings; and after-tax profits equals investment + government purchases – wage taxes – profit taxes + consumption out of profits – worker savings.

Making a number of rather stringent assumptions (including that the economy is operating in a short-period setting with investment fixed, a balanced budget constraint, no foreign sector, no worker savings, and that tax receipts are spent on the unemployed or on government officials who spend all their income), Kalecki showed that introducing a consumption tax on wage goods would not affect the level of gross (pre-tax) profits. In addition, introducing an income tax on capitalist incomes would increase gross profits, and introducing a capital tax on all forms of capital increase profits and employment. This is as far as Kalecki went.

Eatwell (1971), and particularly Asimakopulos and Burbidge (1974), extended Kalecki's analysis considerably, although within the same short-period framework where changes in productive capacity can be ignored because these changes are small. They emphasized the important Post Keynesian distinction between the propensities to save out of wages and out of profits, and analyzed situations of short-period equilibrium where predetermined investment is realized and is equal to what individuals and firms have chosen to save in the period under consideration. Asimakopulos and Burbidge showed that if the government announces and implements a higher tax on profits at the beginning of the short period and spends the extra revenue obtained from the tax increase, post-tax profits will be unaffected by the tax if short-period equilibrium is re-established. Their results hold in both competitive (variable-price) and non-competitive (fixed-price) market conditions. The balanced budget multiplier plays an important role in their analysis.

The Asimakopulos–Burbidge contribution advanced Post Keynesian theory considerably. But with its emphasis on short-period equilibrium, the analysis was more Keynesian than Kaleckian and did not sit comfortably with more general Post Keynesian suspicions of the short period.

If Post Keynesian theory is to analyze the long period, dynamic incidence of taxation, the effects of taxation on investment have to be analyzed. One approach for doing this involves going back to Kalecki's 1937 theory of taxation and integrating it with other elements of Kaleckian economics. Kalecki never attempted this and, in fact, generally abstracted from taxation and government activity in his analysis. However, a major benefit of integrating taxation into the corpus of Kaleckian theory will be to ensure proper congruence of the micro- and macroeconomic foundations, thereby addressing one of the principal weaknesses of neoclassical theory.

Laramie (1991) took a significant step in the integration of taxation into Kalecki's wider theory. Kalecki (1954) showed that the distribution of value added depends on business markups (among other things). Defining value added as profits plus wages (where profits are a markup of over prime costs), Kalecki showed that the wage share was $1/[(k - 1)(1 + j) + 1]$, where k equals the markup and j equals the ratio of the wage bill to the material bill. Assuming businesses do not treat profit taxes as a prime cost (and assuming that businesses do not use full cost pricing), the extent to which a tax affects the wage share depends upon the extent to which a tax alters the business markup, k. For example, an increase in a wage tax, if shifted, results in a reduction in business markup; and an increase in a profits tax, if shifted, results in an increase in business markups. In case of a profits tax, the tax can be shifted forward via a higher price relative to prime costs, or shifted backwards via lower prime costs relative to price.

For Kalecki, the wage share is important in determining the level of national income. Gross profits are determined by the spending flows described in the profit identity and national income is pushed up so that gross profits (as determined by those spending flows) are realized. Consequently, a higher wage share requires a higher level of national income (and employment) given spending flows that determine profits and vice versa. Shifting a wage tax thus increases national income and shifting a profits tax reduces national income given the spending flows that determine aggregate profits. If no tax shifting is present and the government maintains a balanced budget (and assuming workers do not save), a wage tax has no effect on pre-tax profits and national income. In contrast, under the same set of assumptions, a profits tax increases gross profits (without altering post-tax profits) and increases national income and employment. Wage tax shifting raises national income while profit tax shifting dampens, to some degree, the positive effect of the tax on national income. The extent to which tax shifting occurs depends on the relative degrees of market power businesses and labor possess, as determined by institutional factors.

Complications arise when workers save, when the government budget deficit is allowed to vary, or when foreign sector flows react to tax changes. Under these circumstances, a multitude of possibilities arise and the exact incidence and effects of various taxes become empirical questions.

In order to analyze the dynamic incidence of taxation it is necessary to link taxation to Kalecki's theories of profits, national income, wage shares, investment, and the business cycle. For Kalecki, everything is driven by what happens to investment. Changes in the structure of taxation today can affect future investment and, thus, future profits. So, how do changes in the structure of taxation, achieved by balanced changes in taxation and government spending, affect investment?

Kalecki (1954; 1962; 1971/68) set forth three variants of his investment theory. His (Kalecki, 1971/1968) 1968 theory proposes two channels by which taxation impacts investment – the rate of depreciation and the level of profits. The rate of depreciation channel operates by altering the relative profitability (after taxes) of new and existing plant and equipment. With technology continually improving through time, higher taxes on profits will lower the real profits on older equipment relative to new equipment and accelerate its obsolescence, thereby encouraging new investment.

The effect of taxation on the level of profits also operates through two channels (ignoring the foreign sector) – its impact on the government budget and its effect on income distribution. The effect via government purchases is the balanced budget multiplier effect. The effect via income distribution depends on whether or not tax shifting occurs as a consequence of firms altering their markups in response to changes in the structure of taxation. The extent to which this will happen depends on the degree of monopoly. Quite different macroeconomic effects occur depending on whether or not tax shifting takes place. Laramie and Mair (2000) discuss how changes in the structure of taxation can affect investment and the business cycle. A balanced budget increase in the wage tax can increase business profits via a decrease in worker savings (some of the wage tax is paid for by a decrease in worker savings). Greater business profits increase investment. The increase in profits is dampened if a wage tax is shifted via an increase in worker savings. An unshifted change in a wage tax has no impact on the rate of depreciation and no affect on the relationship between real income and profits (in other words, it does not affect the real wage bill). An unshifted increase in a wage tax, therefore, increases the amplitude of the business cycle.

A balanced budget increase in the profits tax reduces after-tax profits via an increase in worker savings and, therefore, reduces investment. Worker savings increase in response to the balanced budget increase in national income and the wage bill. Shifting a profits tax reduces the wage share and wage bill and, therefore, reduces worker savings and dampens the initial reduction in profits and investment. With no tax shifting, an increase in a profits tax increases national income relative to profits (increases the wage bill) and heightens the rate of depreciation. Increased depreciation results in new fixed investment. If a profits tax is shifted, the depreciation effect is dampened. With no tax shifting, the increase in a profits tax dampens the amplitude of the business cycle, while the depreciation effect increases the amplitude of the business cycle. The exact impact of the profits tax on investment, on future profits, and on the amplitude of the business cycle depends upon the relative sizes of these opposing effects and the degree of tax shifting.

This section has shown that fiscal policy can have profound affects in terms of modifying both cyclical and long-term behavior. The Kaleckian approach marks a complete break from conventional Keynesian stabilization policy, which has fallen into disrepute. Above all, it underlines the necessity of considering the effects of tax-induced changes on income distribution.

Illustrations of Post Keynesian tax incidence theory

Post Keynesian tax incidence theory has had a number of interesting applications. On the issue of the effect of taxation on investment, Laramie *et al.*

(1997) have shown that for the US, over the period 1983–93, changes in average wage rates have swamped the effects of changes in average profits tax effects. This conclusion undermines the neoclassical position on three counts. It shows that (1) average tax rates do matter; (2) the economic incidence of taxation must be explicitly considered when considering the effectiveness of tax incentives; and (3) equity considerations need not be subordinated to efficiency objectives. Redistributing income through the tax system may actually increase the profitability of investment, depending on the government budget stance. For example, a more progressive personal income tax, coupled with a government transfer to low-income individuals, can increase (non-wage) consumption relative to the wage bill and increase profits. Despite an increase in profits, Post Keynesians recognize that economic solutions to the problem of uneven economic development and growth might encounter political opposition (Kalecki, 1943).

Laramie and Mair (1996) developed a Post Keynesian approach to state and local taxation. Fiscal policy discussions in the US typically emphasize the role of the Federal Government and downplay the role of state and local governments. The fiscal policies of any one state or locality are thought to have only a marginal impact on the performance of the economy as a whole. However, state and local government receipts and expenditures represent a significant share of GDP (gross domestic product), thereby having a significant affect on aggregate spending and economic growth. The mobility of capital in response to state and local profit taxes is usually seen as the main reason that state and local governments rely on regressive forms of taxation. This, combined with the tendency of state and local governments to run budget surpluses, tends to reduce economic growth and lower profits. Thus Federal Government deficits, grants-in-aid, and progressive taxation are required to promote profits and growth.

The Post Keynesian approach also provides a basis to analyze the macroeconomic effects of taxation after European Union. The Treaty of Maastricht established four convergence criteria for adopting a single currency and full economic and monetary union. These criteria relate to (1) price stability; (2) exchange rate stability; (3) convergence of long-term nominal interest rates; and (4) sustainability of a country's public finance situation. These conditions attempt to reconcile two conflicting issues. On the one hand, the creation of a European Central Bank and the introduction of the single European currency (the Euro) will result in a loss of national monetary autonomy that will need to be compensated by greater fiscal flexibility. On the other hand, the whole thrust of European fiscal policy has been towards fiscal harmonization.

Post Keynesian analysis shows that stabilization under economic and monetary union need no longer depend on the application of orthodox Keynesian fiscal policy (Laramie and Mair, 1997). Balanced changes in the structure of taxation could produce the desired macroeconomic effects. The *quid pro quo* has to be a relaxation of the pursuit of fiscal harmonization so that participating countries can retain the necessary fiscal flexibility.

Conclusion

The Post Keynesian theory of tax incidence is still in its infancy, and much work remains to bring it to maturity. At the microeconomic level, the distributional effects of taxation need to be more fully understood. Work thus far simply accounts for the distributional effects of taxation through a shift parameter in the markup function. Nothing has yet been said about the dynamic nature of wage or profit tax shifting, or about how tax shifting impacts income distribution or aggregate spending. At the macroeconomic level, we must better understand the effects of taxation (and tax shifting) on the various spending flows that influence national income and gross profits. In particular, we need empirical evidence about the exact relationship between the structure of taxation and spending flows. Moreover, the work developed thus far has completely abstracted from relationships between the structure of taxation and foreign sector flows and between fiscal and monetary policy. Finally, we have only considered wage and profit taxes. In the real world a larger multitude of taxes exist.

In short, the incidence of various taxes must be understood in the context of a fully developed Post Keynesian economic model. A full economic model is needed to understand tax incidence because of the important feedback effects stemming from taxation in a world where aggregate demand matters. The effect of taxation on relative prices and distribution only tells part of the story. To complete the story, we need to understand more fully how the tax structure affects aggregate demand.

References

Atkinson, A.B. and Stiglitz, J.E. (1980) *Lectures on Public Economics*, Maidenhead: McGraw-Hill.

Asimakopulos, A. (1978) "Tax Incidence," in A.S. Eichner (ed.) *A Guide to Post Keynesian Economics*, New York: M.E. Sharpe, pp. 61–70.

Asimakopulos, A. and Burbidge, J. (1974) "The Short Period Incidence of Taxation," *Economic Journal*, 84: 267–88.

Blundell, R., Bond, S., Devereux, M. and Schianterelli, F. (1992) "Investment and Tobin's Q," *Journal of Econometrics*, 51: 233–57.

Brainard, W. and Tobin, J. (1968) "Pitfalls in Financial Model Building," *American Economic Review*, 58: 99–123.

Burbidge, J. (1976) "Internally Inconsistent Mixtures of Micro- and Macro-theory in Empirical Studies of Profits Tax Incidence," *Finanzarchiv*, 35: 218–34.

Chirinko, R. (1993) "Business Fixed Investment Spending: Modeling Strategies, Empirical Results and Policy Implications," *Journal of Economic Literature*, 31: 1875–911.

Eatwell, J. (1971) "On the Proposed Reform of the Corporation Tax," *Bulletin of the Oxford Institute of Economics and Statistics*, 33: 267–74.

Harberger, A.C. (1962) "The Incidence of the Corporation Income Tax," *Journal of Political Economy*, 70: 215–41.

Kalecki, M. (1937) "A Theory of Commodity, Income and Capital Taxation," *Economic Journal*, 47: 444–50.

Kalecki, M. (1943) "Political Aspects of Full Employment," *Political Quarterly*, 14: 347–56.

Kalecki, M. (1954) *Theory of Economic Dynamics*, London: Unwin University Books.

Kalecki, M. (1962) "Observations on the Theory of Growth," *Economic Journal*, 72: 134–53.

Kalecki, M. (1971/68) "Trend and the Business Cycle," in *Selected Essays on the Dynamics of the Capitalist Economy*, Cambridge: Cambridge University Press, pp. 165–83.

Keynes, J.M. (1936) *The General Theory of Employment, Interest and Money*, New York: Harcourt Brace.

Kotlikoff, L. and Summers, L. (1987) "Tax Incidence," in A.J. Auerbach and M.J. Feldstein (eds.) *Handbook of Public Economics*, vol. II, Amsterdam: North Holland, pp. 1043–92.

Laramie, A.J. (1991) "Taxation and Kalecki's Distribution Factors," *Journal of Post Keynesian Economics*, 14: 583–95.

Laramie, A.J. and Mair, D. (1996) "The Short Period Macroeconomic Incidence and Effects of State and Local Taxes," in G. Pola, G. France and R. Levaggi (eds.) *Developments in Local Government Finance: Theory and Policy*, Aldershot: Edward Elgar, pp. 135–56.

Laramie, A.J. and Mair, D. (1997) "The Macroeconomic Effects of Taxation in a Federal Europe," in P. Arestis and M. Sawyer (eds.) *The Relevance of Keynesian Economic Policies Today*, London: Macmillan, pp. 1–27.

Laramie, A.J. and Mair, D. (2000) *A Dynamic Theory of Taxation: Integrating Kalecki into Modern Public Finance*, Cheltenham: Edward Elgar.

Laramie, A.J., Mair, D., Miller, A. and Stratopulous, T. (1997) "The Impact of Taxation on Gross Private Non-residential Fixed Investment in a Kaleckian Model: Some Empirical Evidence," *Journal of Post Keynesian Economics*, 19: 243–56.

Musgrave, R. (1997) "Micro and Macro Aspects of Fiscal Policy," in M. I. Blejer and T. Ter-Minassian (eds.) *Macroeconomic Dimensions of Public Finance*, London: Routledge, pp. 13–26.

Stern, N. (1992) "From the Static to the Dynamic: Some Problems in the Theory of Taxation," *Journal of Public Economics*, 47: 273–97.

6 Uncertainty and expectations

J. Barkley Rosser Jr

Introduction

Uncertainty and expectations were both central concerns for Keynes, so it is curious that the first *Guide to Post Keynesian Economics* (Eichner, 1978) had no chapter on this topic. Two factors may help explain this.

First, for Keynes uncertainty was not quantifiable. Tobin (1959), however, hijacked Keynesian uncertainty and turned it into quantifiable risk. This violated the division between measurable risk and immeasurable uncertainty introduced by Frank Knight (1921). Although risk and uncertainty are not identical concepts, Tobin made it seem acceptable to treat them as if they were. Many authors used the term "uncertainty," which is non-quantifiable in the view of Keynes and Post Keynesians economists, and discussed it in terms of objectively measurable and quantifiable risk. This was especially true of financial economists, who incorporated this approach into a model assuming rational expectations and efficient markets, despite Tobin's own skepticism regarding these matters (Weisman, 1984).

Second, when most of the *Guide* was written in the mid-1970s, few economists regarded the idea of rational expectations as important. Muth (1961) introduced the concept of rational expectations and Lucas (1972) applied it to macroeconomics. Lucas used rational expectations to argue against employing policy to improve economic outcomes because people will take into account the actions of the government and act in ways to nullify anything the government tries to do, based on their ability to forecast accurately what the economy will be like in the future. In the late 1970s and early 1980s this "new classical" view, with its *laissez-faire* implications, swept the economics profession and became the main approach in macroeconomics, especially in the US.

Before 1979 Post Keynesians did not feel the need to respond seriously to this idea, as it seemed patently ridiculous. Although some Post Keynesians worried about uncertainty in the original Keynesian sense prior to 1979 (Shackle, 1955, 1972; Kregel, 1976; Loasby, 1976; Davidson, 1978), they felt no need to critique the rational expectations assumption on the grounds of Keynesian uncertainty.

The dominance of rational expectations since the early 1980s has forced Post Keynesians to analyze more systematically the concepts of uncertainty and expectations. This work has made it clear that to combat the rational expectations/new classical policy argument that nothing can (or should) be done to improve economic performance, we need a better understanding of how people form expectations. It also opened the door for a reconsideration of the old view of uncertainty as fundamental and unquantifiable. In this way, Keynes's view of uncertainty undermines the foundation of rational expectations and the policy arguments that flow from it. This chapter examines what Post Keynesians have come to think about this matter.

Keynes on uncertainty and expectations

How people form expectations matters for economics because people act based on what they think is going to happen in the future. Rational expectations provides an appealing answer to this problem because it is simple and grants great insight into economic agents – what people expect will really happen on average. This makes people insightful, and it allows the theorist to impose a view of reality and say that people understand it and expect what the theory forecasts. The assumption that people expect what the theorist says will happen reinforces the forecast that it will happen. People do what the theorist says they will because they know that the theorist is right; and in doing what the theorist says they make the theorist right. Following Lucas, the rationally expected outcome will be a full employment nirvana, because rational workers will always prefer low wages to no wages (and being unemployed) and will accept lower wages unless the government fools people about the future through its arbitrary policy actions. Lucas argued that people cannot be fooled continually, and that his view of expectations overthrew the policy arguments of Keynes.

It is understandable that Post Keynesians would respond to such an argument by going back to Keynes and searching for a critique of this view of expectations formation. Post Keynesians thus rediscovered Keynes's idea that the flighty bird of real capital investment is not driven by long-run rational expectations, but rather by subjective and ultimately irrational "animal spirits," a spontaneous urge to act in the face of uncertainty.

Keynes presented his most extensive thoughts about uncertainty in the *Treatise on Probability* (1921), and he made further remarks in *The General Theory*. The link with expectations comes in Chapter 12 of *The General Theory*, where unquantified uncertainty causes people to look to the current facts and the average state of opinion (the state of confidence) when forming their expectations. People base their expectations on what they place importance on, a point that we shall return to later.

But while the state of long-term expectations may remain steady for long periods, it is also subject to sudden and violent shifts. These shifts are caused by speculation (sometimes irrational) in markets as well as psychological shifts. Keynes (1936: 161) argues that "animal spirits" lie behind capital investment, "a spontaneous urge to action rather than inaction, and not as the outcome of a weighted average of quantitative benefits multiplied by quantitative probabilities." He (1936: Ch. 13) also argues that uncertainty about the future of interest rates underlies liquidity preference and thus constitutes part of the demand for money as well.

Keynes's views on uncertainty have generated much controversy. One reason for this is that Keynes presented several different arguments regarding uncertainty, and he may have shifted his view over time and put more emphasis on its absolutely unquantifiable nature. However, the place to start is the *Treatise on Probability*, where Keynes (1921: 33) distinguishes four cases: there are no probabilities at all (fundamental uncertainty); there may be some partial ordering of probable events but no cardinal numbers can be placed on them; there may be numbers but they cannot be discovered for some reason; and there may be numbers but they are difficult to discover.

The first case describes economic matters taking place far into the future. These outcomes are things we cannot attach any probability to at all. Explaining the difference between what is probable and what is uncertain Keynes (1937: 113) declares:

> The game of roulette is not subject, in this sense to uncertainty; nor is the prospect of a Victory bond being drawn. Or, again, the expectation of life is only slightly uncertain. Even the weather is only moderately uncertain. The sense in which I am using the term is that in which the prospect of a European war is uncertain, or the price of copper and the rate of interest twenty years hence, or the obsolescence of a new invention, or the position of private wealth owners in the social system in 1970. About these matters there is no scientific basis on which to form any calculable probability whatever. We simply do not know.

The second case is associated with the problem of non-comparability or incomplete ordering. Keynes (1921: Ch. 3) argues that some series of possible events may be ordinally ranked with respect to each other in terms of greater or lesser probability, but without any cardinality assigned to these probabilities. Another series of events may also be so ranked among themselves, but no possible event from this series can be compared with any possible event from the first series.

The third case is not explained by Keynes. It possibly reflects Knight's (1921) view that uncertainty is objective but non-quantifiable (Lawson, 1988). The fourth case represents epistemological problems of how to know what we know, whose causes may be many. This case has been debated at length by Post Keynesian economists. A few simple examples would be cases where probabilities are hard to observe, or generate data that is hard to measure or estimate, or when there are too few cases to meaningfully estimate such probabilities.

It should be made clear that Keynes recognized the possibility of quantifying fairly exact probabilities for certain kinds of events, such as the classic examples of flipping coins and rolling a die. He accepts that in some situations insurance companies can make such quantifiable calculations; yet, in other cases, their estimates are essentially arbitrary guesses.

Keynes viewed probability as fundamentally subjective, something that can be constructed from internal logic rather than from mathematical calculations of distributions from external observations. Events are viewed in comparison with each other by their "probability relation," possibly immeasurable. He even raises the problem of induction for cases where *a priori* knowledge and logic might yield something that appears to be a definitive quantitative answer. For example, a fair die will have a one-sixth probability of landing on each side. But how do we know it is a fair die, especially if one side comes up regularly more than the others?

Keynes's subjectivism is more radical and more uncompromising than most other subjectivists, such as Savage (1954), who sees a frequency underpinning to the subjective probabilities assigned by agents. Usually subjective and objective probabilities converge as the number of observations increases – a kind of foreshadowing of rational expectations that assumes an ultimate validity to the concept of objective probability. Keynes rejects this ultimate objectivity, despite accepting that logical deductions can result in reasonable quantified probabilities some of the time. This subjectivism carries over into his views on expectations formation and economic decision-making. There is no way Keynes would have accepted Muth's (1961: 316) view that expectations are rational in the sense that "expectations of firms (or more generally the 'subjective' probability of outcomes) tend to be distributed, for the same information set, about the prediction of the theory (or the 'objective' probability distribution of outcomes)."

As noted above, Keynes suggested that agents form expectations based on how much weight they put on different possibilities. Weight is identified with the amount of relevant evidence someone has gathered regarding the probability of a possible outcome. It is not the same as the probability of that outcome. While it might be tempting to identify this concept with statistical significance in classical statistics, Keynes also rejects the quantitative comparison of such "weights." However, he does emphasize that determining "degrees of belief" is a rational and logical process (O'Donnell, 1990). Later, Keynes (1931: 336–9), moved from a view that probability is an objective relation between propositions (subjectively known through logic) to a view that probability is mostly about "degrees of belief." And those beliefs, which can change suddenly, are strongly influenced by current reality, whose salience impresses and thus contributes greatly to "weight," at least for a time.

Post Keynesian perspectives on uncertainty and expectation

Post Keynesians have drawn on several different viewpoints in developing their position on the nature of uncertainty and expectation formation. One line of argument focuses on the element of potential surprise associated with crucial decisions such as major capital investments. Followers of this line also emphasize the unidirectional and irreversible nature of historical time. Another approach argues that fundamental uncertainty derives from the non-ergodicity of time series and stochastic processes. A third approach emphasizes the interaction of people in forming expectations and the various complexities of group dynamics. Here, expectations are seen as arising from bounded rationality and conventions.

Potential surprise and history versus equilibrium

The implications of non-quantifiable uncertainty were first developed by Shackle (1955, 1972). Along with Loasby (1976), Shackle took an uncompromising stance regarding the ontological[1] nature of Keynesian uncertainty and emphasized its role in the unpredictability and variability of investment. He saw uncertainty as tied to the creativity and free will of the investor, his or her ability to create a new reality that constantly upsets previous realities as "potential surprises" emerge. As a result, Shackle (1974) came to reject the concept of equilibrium and declared that reality is "kaleidic," constantly changing and swirling like the colors of a kaleidoscope.

Shackle (1969) argued that potential surprise lay at the basis of creative decision-making by firms. Others attempted to formalize this idea. Vickers (1978), for example, postulated "surprise functions" and "attractiveness functions" that represent their "attention-commanding" power. This draws decision-makers to focus upon different potential surprises as the basis for behavior.

Running through the arguments of Shackle, Loasby, and Vickers is an emphasis on the unidirectional nature of time, the significance of this for the unknowability of the future, and the ontological nature of uncertainty. Bausor (1982/83) draws into the argument an emphasis on the irrevocability of decisions. As Joan Robinson (1974) noted, there is a big difference between historical time and logical time. For Robinson actual, non-repeatable, historical time has little relation to the abstract time appearing in most theoretical economic equilibrium models. For Bausor, this reinforces the kaleidic vision of Shackle.

Non-ergodicity and uncertainty

The claim that non-ergodicity is endemic to economic systems has also been used to support Keynesian uncertainty. Davidson (1982/83, 1991, 1994, 1996) argues that an ergodic process is one for which time and space averages are equal; what happens at points in time for different initial states coincides with what happens over time for a given initial state. Such stochastic processes (randomly driven dynamic systems) are stationary. This stationarity suggests that economic processes over time follow averages that can be discovered by rational agents, thus implying the possibility of rational expectations. While Keynes was unaware of this concept, Davidson interprets his arguments for uncertainty as implying non-ergodicity and thus widespread non-stationarity of economic time series. For Davidson this becomes a battle-axe to attack the rational expectations hypothesis.

One problem that arises from emphasizing uncertainty is how there can be any predictability regarding policy outcomes if there is such profound uncertainty. Going even further, Coddington (1982) argues that the logic of Keynesian uncertainty leads to nihilism. Davidson (1996) responds to this by citing Shackle (1955) on "cruciality." Potential surprise and non-ergodicity arise only with "crucial" decisions, such as major capital investments or the choice of a career for an individual. Routine decisions may be governed by ergodicity and are somewhat predictable, including much of consumption behavior. On the other hand, the essential creativity of the capital investment process is inherently surprising and non-ergodic.

The issue of stationarity has attracted a good deal of attention from time-series macroeconometricians. Many studies have found unit roots in macroeconomic variables, which implies level non-stationarity, although unit roots can be consistent with trend stationarity, which would seem to violate the spirit of Keynesian uncertainty. A unit root exists when a change in a variable persists and the variable does not return to its previous value.

There have also been efforts to model surprising events using leptokurtosis, or fat-tailed distributions. It is now a stylized fact that most time series of asset prices exhibit such leptokurtosis (Loretan and Phillips, 1994). Such models still assume some kind of stationarity of the mean, which would lead Davidson to argue that they are not truly Post Keynesian because they contain an element of ergodicity. In the case of asymptotically infinite moments there is a violation of ergodicity, strictly speaking. With regard to the criterion of Davidsonian non-ergodicity such cases must be viewed as somewhat ambiguous.

Finally, there has been emphasis on regime switching (Flood and Garber, 1994). This implies that there are periods of "routine" behavior during which ergodicity and predictability may hold; but then "crucial" decisions are made that move the system to another position or another regime in an unpredictable manner. However, there are key differences between the Flood and Garber approach and that of Davidson. First, Flood and Garber emphasize government policies rather than private capital investment as the source of regime switches. Furthermore, they argue that market agents attempt to forecast regime switches in futures markets, although they are not always successful. This approach thus fails to hold that uncertainty is ontological and unavoidable as do most Post Keynesians, and it seems inconsistent with Post Keynesian thought when it argues that uncertainty can be eliminated if governments maintain widely known and time-consistent policies.

Group dynamics

While discussing "The State of Long-Term Expectation" Keynes (1936) gives numerous examples where expectations about others' expectations are crucial. Agents closely watch the "average state of expectations" in forming their own expectations, if for no other reason than if they are wrong they can point to the fact that most others were wrong in order to avoid blame for their mistakes. The most famous example of this interaction is the "beauty contest" example (Keynes, 1936: 156):

> [P]rofessional investment may be likened to those newspaper competitions in which the competitors have to pick out the six prettiest faces from a hundred photographs, the prize being awarded to the competitor whose choice most nearly corresponds to the average preferences of the competitors as a whole; so that each competitor has to pick, not the faces which he himself finds prettiest, but those which he thinks likeliest to catch the fancy of the other competitors, all of whom are looking at the problem from the same point of view. It is not a case of choosing those which, to the best of one's judgment are really the prettiest, nor even those which average opinion genuinely thinks the prettiest. We have reached the third degree where we devote our intelligences to anticipating what average opinion expects our average opinion to be. And there are some, I believe, who practise the fourth, fifth and higher degrees.[2]

Several Post Keynesians (Carabelli, 1988; Davis, 1994; Arestis, 1996) see uncertainty about others' expectations as the fundamental source of general uncertainty. Since we can never know for sure at what "degree" other people will be thinking about how average opinion will form expectations, we can never know for certain other peoples' expectations of average opinion. Since people depend on each other when forming their expectations, sudden mass changes of these expectations, or "mob psychology," are possible.

This vision of the interaction of the expectations of different people leading to sudden and unpredictable changes in group dynamics has inspired an enormous literature in several areas. One has been the topic of speculative bubbles in asset markets. People bid up the price of an asset because they expect that other people will also do so. This can become a self-fulfilling prophecy, at least for awhile. Such behavior may even be rational in some sense, although the literature tends to emphasize the "irrational fad" element of such behavior. Speculation also can lead to the proliferation of new assets (Carter, 1991/92), which may induce greater uncertainty rather than reduce it (Bowman and Faust, 1997).

Another approach along this line has been sunspot equilibrium theories (Azariadis, 1981; Cass and Shell, 1983). According to this approach, agents respond to some "extrinsically uncertain" event (sunspots, the Oracle of Delphi's predictions) to believe or not believe in some outcome. This then becomes a self-fulfilling prophecy. Some of this literature departs from Keynesian uncertainty by positing that the extrinsic event may obey some known probability distribution. For this reason, Davidson (1996) has dismissed such models as a variety of theories where reality is unknown in the short-run because of some epistemological difficulty, thus corresponding to Keynes's fourth case of potentially learnable probabilities that are not easily learned. Nevertheless, this approach has the potential for modeling the arbitrariness of social choice when the extrinsic process is unknown.

Sunspot models generally exhibit multiple equilibria, depending on the state of expectations. A related literature has focused on the problem of coordinating expectations in order to select among equilibria (Cooper and John, 1988; Guesnerie, 1993). Again, Davidson (1996) dismisses this approach because of the epistemological problem of finding a self-adjusting immutable equilibrium; but the openness of the system to the essentially arbitrary choices of the agents suggests that this is not necessarily the case.

A natural extension of these models concerns the adjustment and learning processes that select one equilibrium from a multiplicity of possible self-fulfilling prophecies. It is now clear that such processes may not converge on any equilibrium, and that they may generate all kinds of instabilities and chaotic dynamics (Brock and Hommes, 1997; Hommes and Sorger, 1998).[3] The tendency to "self-fulfilling mistakes" has led Grandmont (1998: 742) to posit an uncertainty principle, "learning, when agents are somewhat uncertain about the dynamics of the economic or social system, is bound to generate local instability of self-fulfilling expectations, if the influence of expectations on the dynamics is significant." This seems to represent the problem that Keynes had in mind when discussing the interaction of peoples' expectations in his beauty contest example.

Conventions and bounded rationality in forming expectations

A close reading of Keynes suggests that people adopt conventions in the face of uncertainty. They attempt to guess the expectations of others until current conditions undermine the convention, the unpredictable impinges upon them, and they must make "crucial" decisions that move things to a different zone. Such a view has recently gained ground against the rational expectations hypothesis. Even Thomas Sargent (1993), an originator of the rational expectations hypothesis, has declared that dynamic complexity implies bounded rationality. Likewise, experimental economics studies and studies from psychology show that people focus on their current environments and are susceptible to the views of those around them. Many of the empirical results of these studies involve anomalies and paradoxes of behavior in which people rather clearly do not follow the predictions of standard neoclassical theory (Kahneman *et al.*, 1982; Thaler, 1994). These studies further emphasize that people do not have some high-level ability to form rational expectations by thinking and weighing all things and options, but instead attempt to learn from the behavior and attitudes of those nearest to them and from the most dramatic or salient events or phenomena that capture their attention, as they are unable to understand everything. They are limited and bounded in what they can perceive and understand.

Although some are unhappy with the idea of bounded rationality, which is associated with models where people optimize their search for information in a world that is costly to learn about, Keynes felt that agents would engage in "rational choice" subject to the information they had and the expectations that they formed, both of which are inevitably bounded. Heiner (1989) argues that this actually induces predictable behavior, as people adopt rules of thumb, or conventions, when a gap emerges between their competence to judge a situation and the difficulty of doing so.[4] When forming these conventions, agents assign "weights" to their observations based on "epistemic reliability" (Gardenfors and Sahlin, 1982). This may lead them to operate with mixtures of conventional probability estimates and conventions for uncertainty. In credit markets this can lead to behaviors that involve both conventional asymmetric information and uncertainty (Dymski, 1994) and may be responsible for financial fragility (Minsky, 1986) due to credit rationing. A variation on this theme is that borrowers and lenders both face fundamental uncertainty. This leads to "asymmetric expectations" that can generate credit rationing and other phenomena in credit markets and macroeconomic fluctuations (Wolfson, 1996).

Ultimately, Post Keynesians must face the implications of the fundamental uncertainty postulated by Keynes. The arguments of Heiner (1989) imply that people will fall back on rules of thumb in moments of great uncertainty. But this is less useful when, as Shackle points out, the crucial decisions of people bring about the uncertainty. There is the threat invoked by Coddington (1982) of a nihilism that keeps us from making any predictions, even for policy. Davidson, who has criticized others for not properly recognizing Keynesian uncertainty, must also face this contradiction when he advocates implementing some beneficial economic policy that requires a degree of forecasting and ergodicity. His response (Davidson, 1996: 506) is to invoke Reinhold Neibuhr's " 'Serenity Prayer': God grant us the grace to accept with serenity the things that cannot be changed (immutable realities), the courage to change things that should be changed (mutable realities), and the wisdom to distinguish the one from the other." Keynes probably would have found the line between these two to be uncertain.

Open questions and policy implications

Keynes viewed probability as a subjective concept that depends on the logical relations between possible events. Since people base their expectations on the weightier of probable events, and since their perceptions depend greatly on other people, expectations can change suddenly and the state of long-term expectation is fundamentally uncertain.

Many issues surrounding this topic remain open to further research and debate within Post Keynesian thought. The fundamental nature of probability and stochastic processes may be the deepest question that is far from closed. How Keynesian uncertainty influences economic decision-making is another issue that requires further investigation. And the problem of how people actually form expectations, what kinds of conventions they use, and how these interact with the institutional structure of the economy must be resolved. However these issues get resolved, one thing that is certain – Keynesian uncertainty is utterly incompatible with the rational expectations hypothesis.

The Post Keynesian perspective on uncertainty and expectations formation is central to the development of Post Keynesian views of macroeconomic policy. Of course, the rejection of rational expectations coincides with a rejection of the "policy ineffectiveness" arguments of the new classical school. The arguments of the New Keynesian school, which emphasize the significance of sticky prices and wages, are also inadequate from a Post Keynesian perspective, as they also draw on rational expectations. Fundamental uncertainty is seen as implying the possibility of long-run unemployment even in a world of perfect competition and fully flexible prices and wages. Uncertainty leads to liquidity preference and the non-neutrality of money in the long run. Most importantly, uncertainty and the associated instability of expectations is seen as underpinning the instability of investment, which is the key cause of macroeconomic fluctuations.

The policy implications arising from these problems certainly include active monetary and fiscal policies. But they also include deeper and more fundamental institutional and structural changes in the economy. Thus, Post Keynesians argue for the development of institutions that can provide more general anchors for making economic decisions. Those that have been suggested include various kinds of incomes policies to stabilize the wage and price process (Lerner and Colander, 1980; Pekkarinen *et al.*, 1992), indicative planning (Frank and Holmes, 1990) to more broadly coordinate expectations formation, and a variety of mechanisms to stabilize investment, including a more substantial role for government in the process of investment.

Government involvement in investment can cover a range of possible activities, including subsidies or public works programs tied to business cycles, to a variety of more direct or indirect methods of controlling investment, including more direct control of the banking system. Keynes (1936: 378) spoke eloquently, although vaguely, on this issue near the end of *The General Theory*:

> Furthermore, it seems unlikely that the influence of banking policy on the rate of interest will be sufficient by itself to determine an optimum rate of investment. I conceive, therefore, that a somewhat comprehensive socialization of investment will prove the only means of securing an approximation to full employment; though this need not exclude all manner of compromises and devices by which public authority will co-operate with private initiative. But beyond this no obvious case is made out for a system of State Socialism which would embrace most of the economic life of the community. It is not the ownership of the instruments of production which it is important for the State to assume. If the State is able to determine the aggregate amount of resources devoted to augmenting the instruments and the basic rate of reward to those who own them, it will have accomplished all that is necessary.

Thus, finally, for Post Keynesians, overcoming the destabilizing tendencies arising from fundamental uncertainty in economic decision-making is probably the central problem facing macroeconomic policy-makers.

Notes

1   "Ontology" refers to the fundamental nature of being or reality. It is often contrasted with "epistemology," the study of knowledge, or how we know that we know something. A view that uncertainty is fundamentally ontological says that it is inherent in the very nature of reality itself. A view that uncertainty is fundamentally epistemological suggests that it is not inherent in the nature of reality itself but only in the limits of our ability to learn about the nature of reality. If only we were smarter or had better access to information, we could overcome uncertainty and achieve either rational or even perfect expectations. Of course, ontological uncertainty implies that there is an epistemological problem that is impossible to overcome.

2   This implies an infinite regress problem in decision-making when one is taking into account the behavior of other agents that can imply undecidability. Conlisk (1996) notes that such infinite regresses can arise when one is contemplating how to economize on information searches or calculations. Is it worth economizing on economizing on economizing .... ? How does one know the optimal stopping point? Or, to put it in terms of the Keynesian beauty contest described above, what is the appropriate "degree" to judge how average opinion forms its expectations about what average opinion will be? This is undecidable and can be viewed as an ontological problem that must be avoided by making a decision intuitively, that is by relying on "animal spirits."

3   Chaotic dynamics involve sensitive dependence on initial conditions so that a small initial error can lead to a wide deviation of outcomes. These have been argued to undermine the possibility of rational expectations (Grandmont, 1985; Rosser, 1991) and to represent an independent source of Keynesian uncertainty (Rosser, 1998; 1999).

4   Others arguing for the emergence of conventions in the face of uncertainty include Carabelli (1988), Carvalho (1988), and McKenna and Zannoni (1993), a view strongly supported in Chapter 12 of *The General Theory* (Keynes, 1936: 152), "In practice we have tacitly agreed, as a rule, to fall back on what is, in truth, a convention."

References

Arestis, P. (1996) "Post-Keynesian Economics: Towards Coherence," *Cambridge Journal of Economics*, 20: 111–35.

Azariadis, C. (1981) "Self-Fulfilling Prophecies," *Journal of Economic Theory*, 25: 380–96.

Bausor, R. (1982/83) "Time and the Structure of Economic Analysis," *Journal of Post Keynesian Economics*, 5: 163–79.

Bowman, D. and Faust, J. (1997) "Options, Sunspots, and the Creation of Uncertainty," *Journal of Political Economy*, 105: 957–75.

Brock, W.A. and Hommes, C.H. (1997) "A Rational Route to Randomness," *Econometrica*, 65: 1059–95.

Carabelli, A. (1988) *On Keynes's Method*, London: Macmillan.

Carter, M. (1991/92) "Uncertainty, Liquidity and Speculation," *Journal of Post Keynesian Economics*, 14: 169–82.

Carvalho, F. (1988) "Keynes on Probability, Uncertainty, and Decision Making," *Journal of Post Keynesian Economics*, 11: 66–81.

Cass, D. and Shell, K. (1983) "Do Sunspots Matter?" *Journal of Political Economy*, 91: 193–227.

Coddington, A. (1982) "Deficient Foresight: A Troublesome Theme in Keynesian Economics," *American Economic Review*, 72: 480–87.

Conlisk, J. (1996) "Why Bounded Rationality?" *Journal of Economic Literature*, 34: 669–700.

Cooper, R. and John, A. (1988) "Coordinating Coordination Failures," *Quarterly Journal of Economics*, 103: 441–65.

Davidson, P. (1978) *Money and the Real* World, 2nd edition, London: Macmillan.

Davidson, P. (1982/83) "Rational Expectations: A Fallacious Foundation for Studying Crucial Decision-Making Processes," *Journal of Post Keynesian Economics*, 5: 182–97.

Davidson, P. (1991) "Is Probability Theory Relevant for Uncertainty," *Journal of Economic Perspectives*, 5(1): 129–43.

Davidson, P. (1994) *Post Keynesian Macroeconomic Theory*, Aldershot: Edward Elgar.

Davidson, P. (1996) "Reality and Economic Theory," *Journal of Post Keynesian Economics*, 18: 479–508.

Davis, J.B. (1994) *Keynes's Philosophical Development*, Cambridge, UK: Cambridge University Press.

Dymski, G. (1994) "Asymmetric Information, Uncertainty, and Financial Structure," in G. Dymski and R. Pollin (eds.) *New Perspectives in Monetary Macroeconomics: Explorations in the Tradition of Hyman P. Minsky*, Ann Arbor: University of Michigan Press, pp. 77–103.

Eichner, A.S. (ed.) (1978) *A Guide to Post Keynesian Economics*, Armonk, NY: M.E. Sharpe.

Flood, R.P. and Garber, P.M. (1994) *Speculative Bubbles, Speculative Attacks, and Policy Switching*, Cambridge: MIT Press.

Frank, J. and Holmes, P. (1990) "A Multiple Equilibrium Model of Indicative Planning," *Journal of Comparative Economics*, 14: 791–806.

Gardenfors, P. and Sahlin, N. (1982) "Unreliable Probabilities, Risk Taking, and Decision-Making," *Synthèse*, 53: 471–87.

Grandmont, J. (1985) "On Endogenous Competitive Business Cycles," *Econometrica*, 53: 995–1045.

Grandmont, J. (1998) "Expectations Formation and Stability of Large Socioeconomic Systems," *Econometrica*, 66: 741–81.

Guesnerie, R. (1993) "Successes and Failures in Coordinating Expectations," *European Economic Review*, 37: 243–68.

Heiner, R.A. (1989) "The Origin of Predictable Dynamic Behavior," *Journal of Economic Behavior and Organization*, 12: 233–58.

Hommes, C.H. and Sorger, G. (1998) "Consistent Expectations Equilibria," *Macroeconomic Dynamics*, 2: 287–321.

Kahneman, D., Slovic, P. and Tversky, A. (eds.) (1982) *Judgment under Uncertainty: Heuristics and Biases*, Cambridge, UK: Cambridge University Press.

Keynes, J.M. [1921] (1973) *Treatise on Probability*, The Collected Writings of John Maynard Keynes, vol. VIII, New York: Macmillan.

Keynes, J.M. [1931] (1973) *Essays in Biography*, The Collected Writings of John Maynard Keynes, vol. X, New York: Macmillan.

Keynes, J.M. (1936) *The General Theory of Employment, Interest and Money*, London: Macmillan.

Keynes, J.M. (1937) "The General Theory of Employment," *Quarterly Journal of Economics*, 51: 209–23.

Knight, F.H. (1921) *Risk Uncertainty and Profit*, Chicago: University of Chicago Press.

Kregel, J.A. (1976) "Economic Methodology in the Face of Uncertainty: The Modelling Methods of Keynes and the Post-Keynesians," *Economic Journal*, 86: 209–25.

Lawson, T. (1988) "Probability and Uncertainty in Economic Analysis," *Journal of Post Keynesian Economics*, 11: 38–65.

Lerner, A. and Colander, D. (1980) *MAP: A Market Anti-Inflation Plan*, New York: Harcourt Brace Jovanovich.

Loasby, B.J. (1976) *Choice, Complexity, and Ignorance*, Cambridge, UK: Cambridge University Press.

Loretan, M. and Phillips, P.C.B. (1994) "Testing the Covariance Stationarity of Heavy-Tailed Time Series," *Journal of Empirical Finance*, 1: 211–48.

Lucas, R.E. Jr (1972) "Expectations and the Neutrality of Money," *Journal of Economic Theory*, 4: 103–24.

McKenna, E.J. and Zannoni, D.C. (1993) "Philosophical Foundations of Post Keynesian Economics," *Journal of Post Keynesian Economics*, 15: 395–407.

Minsky, H.P. (1986) *Stabilizing an Unstable Economy*, New Haven: Yale University Press.

Muth, J.F. (1961) "Rational Expectations and the Theory of Price Movements," *Econometrica*, 29: 315–35.

O'Donnell, R.M. (1990) "Keynes on Mathematics: Philosophical Foundations and Economic Applications," *Cambridge Journal of Economics*, 14: 29–47.

Pekkarinen, J., Pohjola, M., and Rowthorn, B. (eds.) (1992) *Social Corporatism: A Superior Economic System?* Oxford: Clarendon Press.

Robinson, J. (1974) *History versus Equilibrium*, London: Thames Papers in Political Economy.

Rosser, J.B. Jr (1991) *From Catastrophe to Chaos: A General Theory of Economic Discontinuities*, Boston: Kluwer.

Rosser, J.B. Jr (1998) "Complex Dynamics in New Keynesian and Post Keynesian Economics," in R.J. Rotheim (ed.) *New Keynesian Economics/Post Keynesian Alternatives*, London: Routledge, pp. 288–302 .

Rosser, J.B. Jr (1999) "On the Complexities of Complex Economic Dynamics," *Journal of Economic Perspectives*, 13(4): 169–92.

Sargent, T.J. (1993) *Bounded Rationality in Macroeconomics*, Oxford: Clarendon Press.

Savage, L.J. (1954) *The Foundations of Statistics*, New York: Wiley.

Shackle, G.L.S. (1955) *Uncertainty in Economics and Other Reflections*, Cambridge, UK: Cambridge University Press.

Shackle, G.L.S. (1969) *Decision, Order and Time in Human Affairs*, 2nd edition, Cambridge, UK: Cambridge University Press.

Shackle, G.L.S. (1972) *Epistemics and Economics: A Critique of Economic Doctrines*, Cambridge, UK: Cambridge University Press.

Shackle, G.L.S. (1974) *Keynesian Kaleidics: the Evolution of a General Political Economy*, Edinburgh: Edinburgh University Press.

Thaler, R.H. (1994) *The Winner's Curse: Paradoxes and Anomalies of Economic Life*, Princeton: Princeton University Press.

Tobin, J. (1959) "Liquidity Preference as Behavior towards Risk," *Review of Economic Studies*, 25: 65–86.

Vickers, D. (1978) *Financial Markets in the Capitalist Process*, Philadelphia: University of Pennsylvania Press.

Weisman, D.L. (1984) "Tobin on Keynes: A Suggested Interpretation," *Journal of Post Keynesian Economics*, 6: 411–20.

Wolfson, M. (1996) "A Post Keynesian Theory of Credit Rationing, "*Journal of Post Keynesian Economics*, 18: 443–70.

7 Labor and unemployment

John E. King

Introduction

In the first *Guide to Post Keynesian Economics,* Eileen Appelbaum (1978: 100) offered a simple and clear summary of the Post Keynesian approach to labor economics. It largely follows Keynes in its approach to the demand for labor, and the segmented labor market theorists in its approach to the supply of labor. A Post Keynesian analysis of this sort leads to a conclusion radically different from the orthodox, neoclassical theory. This is that neither the demand for labor nor the supply of labor depends on the real wage. It follows from this that the labor market is not a true market, for the price associated with it, the wage rate, is incapable of performing any market-clearing function, and thus variations in the wage rate cannot eliminate unemployment.

There is little or nothing here that a twenty-first century Post Keynesian would find objectionable. But the world has changed since 1979, and mainstream economic theory has changed with it. Mass unemployment has plagued most developed countries, and there has been a dramatic growth in earnings inequality, reversing a long trend towards greater equality (see Chapter 4). Trade unions are on the defensive all over the world, as employers and governments have become more hostile to organized labor. Finally, neoclassical labor economics has become both more sophisticated and cruder. When efficiency wage theorists rediscovered some long-forgotten truths concerning the positive connection between pay and productivity (Stiglitz, 1987), neoclassical theory became more sophisticated. When macroeconomic dimensions disappeared from its analysis of wages and unemployment, and when it insisted on flexibility and deregulation as preconditions for lower unemployment (OECD, 1994), neoclassical theory became cruder. As we shall see, Post Keynesian labor economics differs sharply from mainstream analysis on both theory and policy alike.

Theoretical foundations

Method

A first, important characteristic of the Post Keynesian approach to labor economics is its distinctive methodological position. Orthodox economists claim that economic analysis must begin with individual maximizing behavior. Closely related to this is the assertion that macroeconomic theory must have microfoundations. Post Keynesians reject both methodological individualism and the priority given to microeconomics over macroeconomics. As Michal Kalecki argued, one could make an equally strong case for the "macrofoundations of microeconomics," since individual decisions are conditioned by the macroeconomic context in which agents operate. Firms and workers will behave quite differently in a situation of mass unemployment compared with the case of full employment. For Post Keynesians neither micro- nor macro-analysis should have logical priority (Kriesler, 1996).

Microeconomics

Post Keynesian methodological concerns lead them to reject the neoclassical view of rational economic man, which is especially unconvincing when applied to the analysis of labor. Post Keynesians do not argue that workers or managers are irrational, simply that the law of the excluded middle does not apply in this instance. Individual behavior is not (or, not always) directed to maximizing a clearly specified objective function subject to known (or, probabilistically known) constraints. Workers do not typically engage in labor market search activity, pursuing marginally better job offers, as in orthodox models of labor supply. To some extent this is due to uncertainty: we live in a non-ergodic world, as Paul Davidson (1994: 89–92) puts it, where the neoclassical axioms of rational choice under conditions of risk simply do not apply. Rationality is bounded and individual behavior is governed by habits, norms, routines, and conventions. People look for a better job only when they are seriously dissatisfied with the one that they have; likewise, employers do not appraise, rank, dismiss, and reappoint their entire labor force at the beginning of each working day.

All this was known to institutionalist labor economists in the 1940s and early 1950s (Kaufman, 1988), with whom the Post Keynesians have strong affinities. Writers like Clark Kerr, Richard Lester, Lloyd Reynolds, and (slightly earlier) Sumner Slichter also rejected the individualism of neoclassical microeconomics on the ground that it neglected the social determinants of workplace behavior. Considerations of emulation and envy on the one hand and of fairness and solidarity on the other hand help explain why individuals join unions, develop commitments to informal work groups, and worry more (as Keynes believed) about relative wages than about the trade-off between leisure and consumer goods.

Post Keynesians also share common ground with radical and Marxian labor theory, especially in the context of the effort bargain. Unit labor costs, by definition, equal the hourly wage divided by hourly output; and hourly output depends (holding capital, land, and technology constant) on the quantity and quality of work performed. This, in turn, is a variable. No job is so completely machine-paced, no worker so completely dominated by the boss, that work effort is irrelevant to the productivity of labor. Thus, there exists a struggle over the pace of work and the tasks that are to be performed. Bluff, deception, bargaining, and conflict are unavoidable in this struggle. Production, in short, is a Hobbesian rather than a Walrasian phenomenon (Bowles, 1985). Maintaining "discipline in the factories" (Kalecki, 1943) is a chronic and crucial problem for capitalist employers. This conditions their perspective on managing labor and affects their attitude to macroeconomic policy. For this reason, as Kalecki noted, full employment is unlikely to be sustained in the long run, since it threatens managerial authority.

These insights have recently been rediscovered by New Keynesian economists, and reissued in neoclassical packaging as efficiency wage theory. Echoing Karl Marx, Shapiro and Stiglitz (1984) demonstrate the necessity for a "reserve army of the unemployed" as a disciplinary device in the struggle over the supply of effort. If effort is costly to workers, and if information is asymmetric, employers can never be certain about the productive potential of their employees. Incentives are therefore required to prevent shirking on the job. The wage rate must encourage effort by imposing significant costs of job loss on any worker who is caught shirking and then dismissed. Given the size of unemployment benefits and the value placed by workers on leisure time, the cost of job loss depends on the expected duration of unemployment. Profit maximization necessitates a reserve army; otherwise the cost of job loss would be negligible. Kalecki's Marxian conclusions thereby find support in neoclassical analysis, and some radical economists have identified a process of convergence between orthodox and labor economics (Green, 1988).

Post Keynesians can agree with much of this, especially the implications of efficiency wage theory: "The Law of Supply and Demand has been repealed. The Law of the Single Price has been repealed. The Fundamental Theorem of Welfare Economics has been shown not to be valid" (Stiglitz, 1987: 41). The law of supply and demand is repealed because rational maximizing behavior by employers and workers will not eliminate unemployment; firms will not accept offers from job seekers wanting to undercut existing wages, for this will reduce effort levels and increase unit labor costs. This dovetails with Post Keynesian skepticism that labor markets will tend to clear in the absence of barriers to competition and institutional rigidities. The law of one price has been repealed because the relationship between wages and productivity may differ from firm to firm, making the cost-minimizing wage different for each one. This reinforces the Post Keynesian emphasis on labor market segmentation and discrimination, and their denial that markets would be perfect in the absence of institutional barriers. Finally, the fundamental theorem of welfare economics is invalid because feelings of fairness and justice influence the supply of effort; it is impossible to separate allocative and distributional issues.

Post Keynesians, however, do not accept efficiency wage theory uncritically. They do not regard it as a substitute for a coherent macroeconomic analysis of employment and unemployment – with effective demand playing a critical role in determining the levels of employment and unemployment. Nor have they found any empirical links between the growth of unemployment since the early 1970s and changes in the relationship between productivity and wages (Sawyer, 1998). The logic of the New Keynesian argument suggests that a "reserve army" is a necessary evil, which should be accepted on efficiency grounds and not eliminated by government intervention (De Vroey, 1998). Post Keynesians take a fundamentally different approach to unemployment policy.

Finally, efficiency wage theory is individualistic; unions play no part, and work groups and collective norms are tangential. Post Keynesians reject the monopoly approach to unions, which views them as cartels restricting labor supply and distorting wage differentials from the pattern that would be found in a (supposedly perfect) non-union labor market.

Appelbaum also noted the irrelevance of neoclassical consumer theory to questions of labor supply. Post Keynesians reject the neoclassical theory of consumer behavior, believing it to be either tautological or empirically misleading. Instead, they prefer an analysis of lexicographic preferences, where income effects are much more important than substitution effects (Lavoie, 1992: Ch. 2). This is especially so for labor supply decisions, which, unlike the textbook consumer choices between tea and coffee, are frequently long-term in nature and subject to a very high degree of uncertainty as to their outcome (Rothschild, 1990). Moreover, the term "labor supply decision" is itself a misnomer. Most jobs are offered on a take-it-or-leave-it basis. Workers have little or no scope to vary hours of work, thereby making marginal trade-offs between income and leisure. There is thus no worker sovereignty corresponding to the (very controversial) notion of consumer sovereignty.

How do Post Keynesians analyze the labor market? As Appelbaum stressed, on the demand side of the market, they recognize that oligopoly is the principal market form and that fixed-coefficient technology better characterizes modern industry than the smooth production functions of neoclassical theory. Under these circumstances, employment will vary simply and directly with the level of output, minimizing the importance of factor substitution in response to relative input price changes and denying the inevitability of a negative relationship between real wages and employment even at the level of the individual firm (see Lavoie, 1992: 225–30).

There is also a considerable Post Keynesian literature on wage differentials, shared with (and to a considerable extent borrowed from) institutional and radical economics (Rebitzer, 1993). While not denying a role to human capital in explaining earnings, Post Keynesians emphasize factors relating to the underlying social and economic structure. Discrimination explains why women and minority workers are paid less than would be expected on the basis of their education, training, and experience. Likewise, workers in peripheral industries, employed by small firms operating in highly competitive product markets, do less well than their colleagues in the capital-intensive, oligopolistic core.

The perfect labor market is a myth. Instead there are a number of distinct market segments, and the links between them (and the corresponding cross-elasticities of demand) are weak. This means that government intervention, or other institutional interference with the market, may bring about big changes in wage differentials with negligible consequences for employment levels. The introduction of equal pay in Australia in the early 1970s provides a good example. Discrimination on grounds of gender was outlawed, and the legislation was enforced by the country's arbitration tribunals. The earnings of women rose dramatically relative to those of men. At the same time, contrary to neoclassical expectations, women's share of total employment increased. This implies that men and women find employment in two distinct segments of the labor market (Gregory and Duncan, 1981).

Macroeconomics

At the most elementary level, neoclassical macroeconomics is contained in the ubiquitous aggregate supply and demand analysis. As shown in Figure 7.1, the aggregate demand for output is a decreasing function of the price level, and the aggregate supply of output an increasing function of price, typically increasing in slope as the price level rises. When equilibrium output falls short of the full employment level, it is because the money wage is too high and the aggregate supply function lies too close to the vertical axis. A reduction in money wages would shift aggregate supply to the right, increasing the equilibrium levels of output and employment. In principle, a similar result could be obtained by stimulating aggregate demand through a cut in tax rates or increased public expenditure. This would shift the aggregate demand function

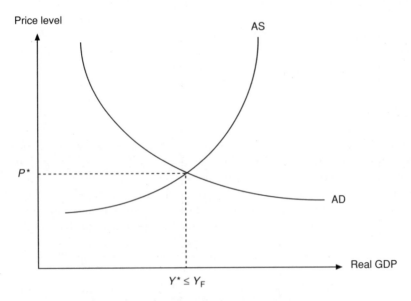

Figure 7.1 A neoclassical model of aggregate supply and demand. P^* = equilibrium price level; Y^* = equilibrium GDP; Y_F = full employment; AD = aggregate demand; AS = aggregate supply.

to the right, but would have unacceptable inflationary consequences. Sustained mass unemployment, on the neoclassical view, can thus be attributed to wage rigidity.

Post Keynesians criticize this analysis on several grounds. First, the aggregate supply function is upward sloping only on the neoclassical assumption of continuously diminishing returns. With fixed-coefficient technology and substantial excess capacity, output can be increased at constant unit cost and aggregate supply will be horizontal over a wide range of output. In Figure 7.2 a reverse L-shaped function illustrates the possibility that output can be increased up to the full employment level with little or no increase in the price level, as occurred in the US during the late 1990s.

Second, Post Keynesians dispute the downward-sloping aggregate demand function. In a closed economy, aggregate demand will increase as the price level falls only if lower prices have a positive wealth effect on consumption (the Pigou effect), or if they reduce the transactions demand for money, leading to lower interest rates and increased investment expenditure (the Keynes effect). In an open economy there is also an international trade effect, since a decline in the price level relative to other countries will increase export demand and reduce imports.

Post Keynesians argue that the Keynes effect will normally be very small.

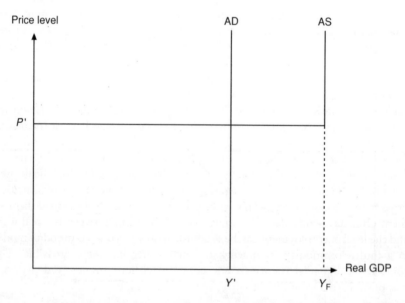

Figure 7.2   A Post Keynesian model of aggregate supply and demand. P' = price level (dependent on money wage level); $Y (< Y_F)$ = real GDP (dependent on aggregate demand); AD = aggregate demand; AS = aggregate supply.

The international trade effect cannot operate in the world as a whole and, except for small open economies, may be very small in magnitude. The Pigou effect may actually be perverse. A decline in the price of assets (especially equities and real estate), and an increase in the real value of debt, may trigger a financial crisis, causing declines in both consumption and investment spending. It follows from this that nothing can be said, in general, about the shape of the aggregate demand curve. Figure 7.2 draws it as a vertical line, on the assumption that the demand-stimulating and demand-depressing effects of changes in the price level cancel each other out.

The policy implications of the Post Keynesian Figure 7.2 differ markedly from those of the neoclassical Figure 7.1. In Figure 7.2, a reduction in money wages reduces the price level but will not increase output or employment. Conversely, an increase in money wages raises the price level and will probably initiate an inflationary wage–price spiral, but it will not reduce output or increase unemployment. A Post Keynesian dualism operates here: output and employment are demand-determined, while (up to full employment) the price level depends only on supply conditions, particularly on the level of money wages (see Moore, 1998). These conclusions follow from the assumptions made in Figure 7.2; but they would not be seriously undermined if the aggregate supply function were drawn as upward sloping over a range of output close to the full employment level.

What about the link between real wages and employment? Mainstream theory asserts a negative relationship, extending its microeconomic analysis to the macroeconomic level. Diminishing marginal productivity gives us a downward-sloping labor demand curve. With an upward-sloping labor supply function, unemployment can be attributed to an excessive real wage. Eliminating unemployment requires lower real wages.

Post Keynesians criticize this on three grounds. First, they reject the neoclassical assumption of diminishing returns as inconsistent with empirical evidence on both production costs at the micro-level and the relationship between employment and output (as summarized in Okun's Law) at the macro-level. Second, even if diminishing returns holds, the direction of causation is the reverse of that in the mainstream argument: for Post Keynesians it is changes in employment that lead to changes in real wages (Riach, 1995). Third, there are intractable problems in aggregating the labor demand curves of individual firms to derive an economy-wide labor demand function. Neoclassical theorists themselves have conceded that a negative relationship between the real wage and the level of employment can be established only in a one-commodity model; in a multi-commodity framework no such generalization is possible. This confines neoclassical theory to an economy without money and makes it inapplicable to a capitalist or entrepreneurial economy.

Policy issues

Unemployment

During the Golden Age of capitalism, from 1945 to about 1973, full employment prevailed throughout the world with only minor exceptions. After 1973 unemployment rose rapidly during recessions but fell back only slightly in the ensuing upswing. Increasing unemployment has thus been the trend. Rising unemployment began later in countries of northern and central Europe that entered the 1970s with effective incomes policies based on corporatist institutions and a high degree of social cohesion (Cornwall, 1994). But, even in these countries, full employment proved unsustainable. The Swedish success story, for example, turned into a disaster over a period of five years, with unemployment rising from 2.1 percent in April 1991 to 10.0 percent in April 1996. Only in the US has unemployment returned to the levels of the late 1960s.

The mainstream response to rising unemployment is summarized in the extremely influential OECD (1994) Jobs Study, which argued that flexible labor markets are the key to increasing employment. In the US (and also in Britain and New Zealand), wage rates were allowed to fall in response to high unemployment. Conversely, in the inflexible, over-regulated labor markets of continental Europe, powerful trade unions and interventionist governments prevented the necessary adjustment processes. The cost was stubbornly high levels of unemployment. The cure, then, is obvious: deregulation, greater wage flexibility, and lower wages, especially for those with few skills.

This story, however, has serious flaws. Deregulation in New Zealand, which halved trade union membership in five years, did not restore full employment. The initial experience of the corporatist countries is also not easy to reconcile with the notion of "Eurosclerosis". As we saw in the previous section, there is also no theoretical reason to expect a negative relationship between employment and the real wage, even at the level of the individual firm. At the macroeconomic level, if a relationship exists between aggregate employment and the real wage, it is employment that determines wages. Employment and unemployment are product market variables, not labor market variables. Thus attempts to restore full employment by cutting wages are fundamentally misguided.

For Post Keynesians, labor market policy is largely irrelevant to solving the unemployment problem. It is the product market that needs fixing, and it needs fixing from the demand side. Post Keynesians conclude that lower real interest rates and higher government expenditure will generate faster growth in output and employment. Increased public sector employment should be carefully targeted to neglected areas of social services and environmental improvement that are not merely labor-intensive, but also low skilled. A strong case can be made for having the state act as "employer of last resort," guaranteeing a public sector job at a socially acceptable minimum wage to all those unemployed for more than a few months and unable to find private sector work (Mitchell and Watts, 1997; Wray, 1998).

If supply-side adjustments are also desirable, they should take the form of an active industry policy to compensate for the private sector's inability to pick winners. International coordination of demand expansion, and controls over currency speculation, will be needed to remove the balance of payments constraint that might otherwise restrict the growth of employment in any individual national economy, and an incomes policy should be used to remove the risk of renewed inflation. Finally, to promote more rapid productivity growth, radical reform of workplace relations and human resources management is needed. Fear of unemployment must be replaced by positive measures of industrial democracy as the principal motivation for commitment to the job. The financial system should be reformed to eliminate discrimination against worker cooperatives, which have a very good record in this regard (Sawyer, 1989: 66–73).

Inequality

In what has been described as a "great U-turn" (Bluestone and Harrison, 1988), the gap between high-paid and low-paid workers in the US began to widen in the 1970s after several decades of increasing equality. A law of the shrinking middle has come to operate: the proportion of workers in highly paid jobs (those earning more than double the median wage) has increased, those in badly paid jobs (earning less than half of the median) has risen rapidly, and there has been a corresponding decline in the proportion in between. This tendency towards increased dispersion in earnings appears to be a global phenomenon. It has occurred not only in countries with highly deregulated labor markets like Britain, but also in Australia, where (until recently) a centralized system of wage determination through compulsory arbitration has operated. The comprehensive study by Gottschalk and Smeeding (1997) found that wage inequality among prime-age men increased during the 1980s in every industrialized economy, with the exception of Germany and Italy. The increase was most rapid in the UK and the US, and slowest in the Scandinavian countries. Three broad explanations have been offered for this phenomenon.

A first explanation emphasizes technical change, which, contrary to the expectations of Marxists like Harry Braverman (1974), has increased the relative demand for highly educated and qualified labor at the expense of the low skilled. This explanation is favored by the majority of neoclassical labor economists.

International trade is a second cause of rising inequality. Adrian Wood (1994) has been the most prominent advocate of the view that trade liberalization and improved communications have increased competition from producers in the South and damaged the labor market position of low-skilled workers in the North. This view that international trade has been the chief cause of increasing inequality is shared by only a small minority of orthodox economists.

A third explanation, emanating from radical theorists, sees sociopolitical factors as more important than either technological change or globalization. The return of mass unemployment, it is maintained, has shifted the balance of power in favor of capital, permitting a sustained and largely successful attack on organized labor and on state protection of wages and working conditions. In the US, union membership declined dramatically, largely as a result of the aggressive anti-union strategies by employers; and the real minimum wage declined between 1980 and 1992 (Mishel and Schmitt, 1995). A similar story can be told for Thatcher's Britain, and it need not be confined to wages. The 1990s saw the growth of "non-standard" employment throughout the world. Unstable, insecure, and precarious jobs are the only ones available to an ever-larger proportion of the labor force, and the consequent growth of temporary, part-time, and casual work has (rather obviously) had a disproportionately large impact on the low paid, and on low-paid women in particular. Flexible work time increasingly operates in the interests of management rather than workers, culminating in some instances in the "zero-hours contract," where workers are required to turn up for work but only get paid when customers arrive and demand service. If capital were weaker, and labor stronger, such just-in-time techniques could not have been extended from the management of inventories to the exploitation of human beings (Campbell and Brosnan, 1999).

These three explanations are not mutually exclusive, and undoubtedly each contains some truth. As for policy, almost no one favors restricting new technology or increasing barriers to trade, although a case can be made for suspending or slowing trade liberalization measures until full employment is restored. Among neoclassical economists there is almost complete unanimity that only human capital improvements (subsidized education and training) are worth serious consideration. Post Keynesian skepticism stems from segmented labor market analysis.

The Post Keynesian alternative has several components; all involve reversing recent policy changes. First and foremost, demand expansion should reduce unemployment and help redress the balance of power between capital and labor. Second, there must be re-regulation of the labor market, including an enforceable charter of worker rights, restoring statutory wage-fixing institutions and maintaining the real value of minimum wage rates. Third, there should be a substantial increase in public employment, including a job guarantee for the long-term unemployed at minimally acceptable rates of pay. Here policy on unemployment and on equality come together (an integrated package for the UK is proposed by Kitson *et al.*, 1997). Fourth, some Post Keynesians are attracted by French initiatives for work-sharing, with a standard thirty-five-hour week and statutory restrictions on overtime working. However, no formal Post Keynesian analysis has yet been done on this possibility.

Unfinished business

There is no reason why Post Keynesian labor economists should adhere dogmatically to the proposition that all unemployment in excess of some very modest frictional minimum is due to inadequate effective demand. It would be wrong to rule out the possibility of a significant increase in structural unemployment, reflected in unfilled job vacancies for which the unemployed are either inappropriately skilled or unsuitably located. This would be reflected in an outward shift in the relationship between unemployment and job vacancies, that is, in the "UV curve" or "Beveridge curve" (named after the British social reformer W. H. Beveridge), as illustrated in Figure 7.3. The curves are simplified versions of econometrically estimated relationships. Their distance from the origin indicates the degree of mismatch between unemployed workers and unfilled vacancies. An outward shift shows that the labor market is less efficient than before in matching jobs with workers.

The empirical evidence, however, fails to support the proposition that increased unemployment since the early 1970s has been largely structural (or frictional) in nature. Beveridge curves have shifted outwards in many countries, but not by very much. Typically, movement has been from A to B in Figure 7.3, but not from A to C. There are relatively few unfilled vacancies; most of the increase in unemployment has been due to deficient aggregate demand.

But we do need to worry more about technological unemployment. Computers have become cheaper relative to labor, and one does not need to be a neoclassical theorist to be concerned about the displacement of human beings by microprocessors (Moore, 1995. A skeptic might reply that "wolf" has been cried on this question too often in the past, and that little hard evidence exists of growing technological unemployment. Productivity growth slowed in the 1970s and 1980s, when the revolution in information technology began, and

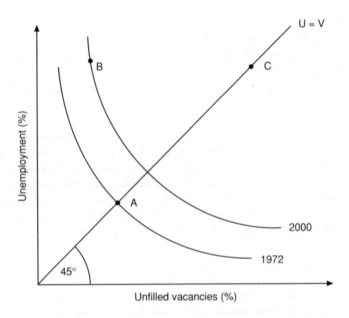

Figure 7.3   Beveridge curves (1972 and 2000). The 45° line, where U = V, shows the full employment condition that *all* unemployment is due to mismatch.

the elasticity of employment with respect to output seems to have increased, rather than declining as one might have expected. Analysis of the relationship between the utilization of capital and the utilization of labor is thus a high priority for future research, along with a detailed investigation of policy options. If the stimulation of effective demand cannot restore full employment, then assuring everyone a basic income, unconditional on work or job search activity, may be the only way to maintain social justice (Van Parijs, 1995).

A second research priority is the labor process. Post Keynesian analysis stresses the distributional conflict between capital and labor and asserts that this conflict can be managed without revolutionary upheaval or socioeconomic disintegration. At the macroeconomic level this leads to the call for an anti-inflationary incomes policy. Just what this means at the level of the individual firm is less clear. Presumably, there must be cooperation between unionized labor and management, with both parties committed to a long-term relationship based on mutual trust and cooperation in the interests of productivity growth and increased job satisfaction. But why, then, have corporations become so anti-union in the last twenty years, placing flexibility above commitment and reasserting the unfettered prerogatives of management?

Union decline has been an international phenomenon, by no means confined to the Anglo-Saxon countries where it seems to have begun. If unions are no longer central to the process of money wage determination, there must be doubts about the relevance of Post Keynesian inflation theory and the associated policy prescriptions. If corporations increasingly behave like ruthless short-run cost minimizers, the Post Keynesian theory of the firm must be reconsidered. Unfortunately, little serious thinking has been done on these issues so far. But policies to combat a short-term perspective in the "market" for labor are no less important than the more frequently discussed policies to discourage short-term perspectives in financial markets.

A third priority is the integration of feminist ideas into Post Keynesian labor economics. Feminists and Post Keynesians have much in common, especially in their criticisms of neoclassical labor economics. Both have far-reaching methodological objections to mainstream ideas, with feminist hostility to "the separative self" (Humphries, 1995: xv) paralleling the Post Keynesian rejection of methodological individualism. Both schools of thought are suspicious of the alleged optimality of unregulated market capitalism. Some substantive feminist concerns are addressed in the Post Keynesian literature on labor, including the issues of discrimination, dual and segmented markets, the endogeneity of tastes, and the denial of worker (and consumer) sovereignty. Feminists would almost certainly claim, with some justice, that a great deal remains to be done. Post Keynesians still tend to accept GDP uncritically as their index of aggregate output, ignoring the (overwhelmingly female) contribution of household labor and domestic production that is omitted from conventional national accounting data. They have also been insufficiently critical of the nexus between work and income, and generally unimaginative in speculating about alternatives, such as basic income.

Summary

Although much remains to be done, Post Keynesians have made substantial progress in criticizing neoclassical orthodoxy, and in offering a distinct and coherent alternative analysis of labor and unemployment. They reject the mainstream insistence on methodological individualism, on constrained maximization as the only way to study the firm, and on the logical priority of the micro over the macro. They are skeptical of the explanatory significance of efficiency wage theory, and instead emphasize the influence of social power, collective action, custom, routine, and institutional constraints on firm and worker behavior.

On policy questions, Post Keynesians argue that unemployment should be tackled via the product market, and deny that it is the result of inflexible labor markets. They call for expanding effective demand rather than reducing wages. Thus Post Keynesians support full employment and a re-regulation of the labor market as essential preconditions for a just and efficient economy.

References

Appelbaum, E. (1978) "The Labor Market," in A.S. Eichner (ed.) *A Guide to Post Keynesian Economics*, London: Macmillan, pp. 100–19.

Bluestone, B. and Harrison, B. (1988) *The Great U-Turn: Corporate Restructuring and the Polarizing of America*, New York: Basic Books.

Bowles, S. (1985) "The Production Process in a Competitive Economy," *American Economic Review* 75(1): 16–36.

Braverman, H. (1974) *Labor and Monopoly Capital*, New York: Monthly Review Press.

Campbell, I. and Brosnan, P. (1999) "Labour Market Deregulation in Australia: The Slow Combustion Approach to Workplace Change," *International Review of Applied Economics*, 13(3): 353–94.

Cornwall, J. (1994) *Economic Breakdown and Recovery: Theory and Policy*, Armonk, NY: M.E. Sharpe.

Davidson, P. (1994) *Post Keynesian Macroeconomic Theory: A Foundation for Successful Economic Policies for the Twenty-First Century*, Aldershot: Edward Elgar.

De Vroey, M. (1998) "Accounting for Involuntary Unemployment in Neoclassical Theory: Some Lessons from Sixty Years of Uphill Struggle," in R. Backhouse, D. Hausman, U. Maki and A. Salanti (eds.) *Economics and Methodology: Crossing Boundaries*, London: Macmillan, pp. 177–224.

Gottschalk, P. and Smeeding, T.M. (1997) "Cross-national Comparisons of Earnings and Income Inequality," *Journal of Economic Literature* 35: 633–87.

Green, F. (1988) "Neoclassical and Marxian Conceptions of Production," *Cambridge Journal of Economics* 12(3): 299–312.

Gregory, R.G. and Duncan, R.C. (1981) "Segmented Labor Market Theories and the Australian Experience of Equal Pay for Women," *Journal of Post Keynesian Economics* 3(3): 403–28.

Humphries, J. (1995) "Introduction," in J. Humphries (ed.) *Gender and Economics*, Aldershot: Edward Elgar, pp. xiii–xxxix.

Kalecki, M. (1943) "Political Aspects of Full Employment," *Political Quarterly* 14(4): 322–31.

Kaufman, B.E. (1988) *How Labor Markets Work: Reflections on Theory and Practice*, Lexington, MA: Lexington Books.

Kitson, M., Michie, J. and Sutherland, H. (1997) " 'A Price Well Worth Paying'? The Benefits of a Full-Employment Strategy," in J. Michie and J. Grieve Smith (eds.) *Employment and Economic Performance: Jobs, Inflation and Growth*, Oxford: Oxford University Press, pp. 234–52.

Kriesler, P. (1996) "Microfoundations: a Kaleckian perspective," in J.E. King (ed.) *An Alternative Macroeconomic Theory: The Kaleckian Model and Post Keynesian Economics*, Boston: Kluwer, pp. 55–72.

Lavoie, M. (1992) *Foundations of Post Keynesian Economic Analysis*, Aldershot: Edward Elgar.

Mishel, L. and Schmitt, J. (1995) (eds.) *Beware the U.S. Model: Jobs and Wages in a Deregulated Economy*, Washington, DC: Economic Policy Institute.

Mitchell, W.F. and Watts, M.J. (1997) "The Path to Full Employment," *Australian Economic Review* 30: 436–44.

Moore, B.J. (1995) "Sluggish Job Growth: Rising Productivity, Anemic Recovery, or Something Else?" *Journal of Post Keynesian Economics* 17: 473–7.

Moore, B.J. (1998) "Money and Interest Rates in a Monetary Theory of Production," in R.J. Rotheim (ed.) *New Keynesian Economics/Post Keynesian Alternatives*, London: Routledge, pp. 339–55.

Organization for Economic Cooperation and Development (1994) *The OECD Jobs Study: Evidence and Explanations. Part 1: Labour Market Trends and Underlying Forces of Change*, Paris: OECD.

Rebitzer, J.B. (1993) "Radical Political Economy and the Economics of Labor Markets," *Journal of Economic Literature* 31: 1394–434.

Riach, P.A. (1995) "Wage-employment Determination in a Post Keynesian World," in P. Arestis and M. Marshall (eds.) *The Political Economy of Full Employment*, Aldershot: Edward Elgar, pp. 163–75.

Rothschild, K.W. (1990) "A Note on Some Socioeconomic and Normative Aspects of Risk," *Review of Political Economy* 2(3): 359–65.

Sawyer, M.C. (1989) *The Challenge of Radical Political Economy*, Brighton: Harvester Wheatsheaf.

Sawyer, M.C. (1998) "New Keynesian Macroeconomics and the Determination of Wages and Employment," in R.J. Rotheim (ed.) *New Keynesian Economics/Post Keynesian Alternatives*, London: Routledge, pp. 118–33.

Shapiro, C. and Stiglitz, J.E. (1984) "Equilibrium Unemployment as a Worker Discipline Device," *American Economic Review* 74: 433–44.

Stiglitz, J.E. (1987) "The Causes and Consequences of the Dependence of Quality on Price," *Journal of Economic Literature* 25(1): 1–48.

Van Parijs, P. (1995) *Real Freedom For All*, Oxford: Clarendon.

Wood, A. (1994) *North–South Trade, Unemployment and Inequality: Changing Fortunes in a Skill-Driven World*, Oxford: Clarendon.

Wray, L.R. (1998) *Understanding Modern Money: The Key to Full Employment and Price Stability*, Cheltenham: Edward Elgar.

8 Money and inflation

L. Randall Wray

Introduction

In his chapter on money in the original *Post Keynesian Guide*, Basil Moore (1978) stressed the importance of historical time and the value of liquidity in an uncertain world. He also set forth the horizontalist approach to money, noting that central banks cannot control the money supply and that money was therefore endogenous. Moore linked money, finance, and investment along the lines suggested by Keynes and Kalecki, and emphasized that the way investment gets financed in a capitalist economy is likely to generate cyclical behavior.

Moore also emphasized that Post Keynesians see inflation as the result of wage growth in excess of productivity growth. This left only three policy alternatives – do nothing and allow inflation to accelerate, raise unemployment to fight inflation, or adopt a tax-based incomes policy.

Most of Moore's analysis has withstood the test of time. This chapter will update and extend his analysis as well as summarize some recent advances. After first examining the orthodox approach to money and inflation, we examine Chartalism, a line suggested by Keynes that has generated recent extensions to the Post Keynesian approach to money. Finally, we look at the current state of Post Keynesian thought on money and inflation in greater detail.

A brief overview of the orthodox approach to money

Modern orthodoxy reaches its highest level of development in general equilibrium theory. The general equilibrium approach assumes perfect competition and perfect knowledge. An auctioneer announces a vector of relative prices for all scarce commodities; individual prices then adjust until all excess demand and supply gets eliminated. At this point all trades occur.

As Hahn (1983) noted, there is no room for money in this sort of economy. Trade takes place via barter. One can choose any commodity to serve as numeraire, giving each commodity a price relative to the numeraire commodity. Nominal prices are rather insignificant here, and money gets introduced only to explain these unimportant nominal prices and inflation.

In the orthodox approach, banks create most of our money, but they are constrained by required reserves of high-powered money. Given a stable deposit multiplier (itself a function of the ratio of reserves to deposits), the supply of deposits will be determined by the quantity of loans demanded and available reserves. Governments control the lending process by dictating reserve ratios and controlling the quantity of reserves. For this reason orthodox monetary theory holds that the money supply is determined exogenously by government policy.

Because of the supposed link between money and inflation, orthodoxy focuses on controlling money growth in order to control inflation. Keeping monetary growth at some low and constant rate, close to the long-run average growth rate of real GDP, ensures long-run stability of the aggregate price level.

After World War II Keynesians and monetarists debated whether the government could closely control money supply growth, and whether money was neutral or not. Keynesians emphasized deposit multiplier instability, and thought monetary policy could not fine-tune real GDP. However, after Brunner (1968) demonstrated that central banks could offset instability in the deposit multiplier by changing aggregate reserves, orthodox economists came to accept the monetarist view that governments could control the money supply. Then rational expectations effectively eliminated any discussion of using monetary policy for short-run fine-tuning. Thus, by the late 1970s, orthodoxy reached a consensus that monetary policy should control the money supply in order to control inflation.

This led to the disastrous Volcker experiment in the US (which was replicated in the UK), in which the Federal Reserve tried to target reserves and hit monetary growth targets. The most surprising results were that the Federal Reserve consistently missed its targets, and that any correlation between money growth and inflation disappeared. By the end of the 1980s all pretense of targeting monetary aggregates was abandoned (Papadimitriou and Wray, 1994). Orthodox economists reluctantly came to the conclusion that money growth and inflation were not linked in any manner that allows for policy formulation. As a result, since the 1990s, monetary policy has shifted away from attempts to control money growth and towards control of inflation by controlling economic growth and unemployment.

Keynes, Knapp, and the neo-Chartalist approach

The orthodox approach emphasizes the medium of exchange function of money. Keynes, however, focused on money as a unit of account and on the role of the state in establishing the money of account. In the *Treatise*, Keynes (1976: 3) claimed that money "can only exist in relation to a money of account," hinting that the unit of account must precede use of a medium of exchange. Elsewhere he (Keynes, 1982: 253) argued that "for most important social and economic purposes what matters is the money of account."

Keynes (1976: 11) also emphasized the role played by the state in first establishing a money of account, "Chartalism begins when the State designates the objective standard which shall correspond to the money-of-account." While

Keynes did not claim that money originated as a state-designated unit of account, he did emphasize that for the past 4,000 years the state claimed "the right to determine and declare what thing [money] corresponds to the name [unit of account], and to vary its declaration from time to time" (Keynes, 1976: 4).

How does a state adopt a unit of account? Schumpeter (1954) and Davidson (1978) emphasize legal tender laws. The state issues a currency, then passes laws requiring that currency be accepted in public and private payments. Knapp, however, doubted that this would be sufficient. In his view, the state determines what will serve as the unit of account when it determines what will be "accepted at public pay offices" (Knapp, 1924: vii–viii, 40). Keynes (1976: 6f.) endorsed this view, as did Lerner (1947: 313), who explained that declarations, alone, will not make something money.

> But if the state is willing to accept the proposed money in payment of taxes and other obligations to itself the trick is done. Everyone who has obligations to the state will be willing to accept the pieces of paper with which he can settle the obligations, and all other people will be willing to accept these pieces of paper because they know that the taxpayers, etc. will accept them in turn.

In the orthodox story, market participants "spontaneously" decide to use some scarce and valuable commodity as a medium of exchange. Neo-Chartalism insists, instead, that the value of money comes from the willingness of the state to accept it in payment for obligations to the state. In a similar vein, Minsky (1986: 231) argued "the fact that taxes need to be paid gives value to the money of the economy. [T]he need to pay taxes means that people work and produce in order to get that in which taxes can be paid."

Thus, those Post Keynesians who accept the neo-Chartalist approach have emphasized that the state chooses the unit of account. It provides moneyness (or liquidity) to those things it accepts as payments, and it ensures that this money will be accepted by imposing money-denominated liabilities (for example, taxes) on the population.

The Post Keynesian approach to money and inflation

The recent contributions to Post Keynesian monetary theory include:

1   attention to Keynesian uncertainty as a major motive for hoarding money;
2   a revival of the monetary theory of production, advanced by Marx and further articulated by Keynes;
3   an analysis of the monetary circuit;
4   a detailed investigation of central bank operations, leading to the "horizontalist" approach that denies reserves are discretionary; and
5   an incomes approach to inflation rather than a monetary approach.

Certainly, this does not exhaust all the Post Keynesian contributions in this area; nor do we wish to suggest that there is no controversy regarding these issues among Post Keynesians. For the most part, we will be brief about the controversies.

Keynesian uncertainty

Uncertainty is dealt with elsewhere in this volume (see Chapter 6), but no discussion of the Post Keynesian approach to money can ignore this topic. Post Keynesians, especially those following Davidson (1978), emphasize that many economic outcomes are non-ergodic, meaning that it is not possible to calculate a probability distribution for alternative events. This is why we use legally enforceable contracts written in the money of account. Holding money always increases liquidity, defined as the ability to meet contractual obligations as they come due.

Post Keynesians also follow Keynes in asserting that money has two special characteristics – a zero elasticity of production (which means that when the demand for money rises, labor is not put to use to produce more of it) and a near-zero elasticity of substitution (when money demand rises, it has no close substitutes to satisfy the demand). These special characteristics, together with existence of Keynesian uncertainty, ensure that money cannot be neutral. When "disquietude" about the future rises, people want more liquidity and money demand rises. Since there are no close substitutes, and because labor will not be directed toward producing more money, the rising demand for liquidity cannot be met.

In an attempt to gain liquidity, people try to sell assets with less liquidity than money has. Asset prices then fall (and interest rates rise) until people become satisfied to hold the existing amount of money. High interest rates cause investment to collapse and also cause output to fall through the multiplier. On the other hand, when people become optimistic about the future, the desire to hold liquidity (money) falls, raising prices of alternative assets (as people try to rid themselves of money by purchasing assets) and lowering interest rates. As demand prices for capital assets rise above the prices required to induce suppliers to produce these assets, more capital is produced. When investment increases, consumption goods output likewise increases through the mechanism of the multiplier. Thus, money is not neutral for Post Keynesians, because the desire for liquidity in an uncertain world generates real effects on production and employment.

This does not imply that the money supply is fixed or exogenous. Keynes himself recognized that when spending increases, the money supply normally expands as banks allow overdrafts. Moore (1988) noted that firms normally negotiate lines of credit, which allow them to increase their borrowing as needed to finance expanded production. On the other hand, when desired spending falls, the supply of loans and the money supply will contract. Thus, the money supply usually expands and contracts endogenously with the business cycle.

Indeed, when expectations about the future collapse and people desire more liquidity, the money supply might actually shrink. Robinson (1979: 157) had argued that expectations count "twice over" when the money supply is endogenous – first because rising uncertainty increases liquidity preference and thus the desire to hold money, and second because these same expectations will reduce desired spending and thus bank loans and deposits. For this reason Wray (1990), Dow and Dow (1989), Dalziel (1996), and others have argued that it is best to distinguish liquidity preference from money demand; the former describes a preference for holding money and other liquid assets (hoarding), whereas the latter describes a desire to obtain money in order to spend it. Rising money demand will normally cause the money supply to expand, while rising liquidity preference will not (and, indeed, may be associated with falling money supply).

A monetary theory of production

Early drafts of the *General Theory* indicate that Keynes was developing a monetary theory of production – a general theory of an economy in which production begins and ends with money. This was similar to Marx's M–C–M' scheme, according to which production begins with money (M), which purchases commodities to produce other commodities (C), which are then sold to realize more money (M', where M' > M if profits are realized). Keynes (1973: 408–9) juxtaposed his approach to the orthodox approach:

> An economy, which uses money but uses it merely as a neutral link between transactions in real things and real assets and does not allow it to enter into motives or decisions, might be called – for want of a better name – a real-exchange economy. The theory which I desiderate would deal, in contradistinction to this, with an economy in which money plays a part of its own and affects motives and decisions and is, in short one of the operative factors in the situation. And it is this which we ought to mean when we speak of a monetary economy.

The monetary theory of production applies to an economy in which money can never be neutral. In contrast, the orthodox view sees money replacing barter without entering into decision processes. The *General Theory* (Keynes, 1964) explained the importance of this distinction: in a monetary economy no forces push the economy to full employment. The special properties of money made it likely that an equilibrium would be achieved at less than full employment, and that the unemployment itself would tend to set in motion processes that move the economy further away from full employment. In contrast, in the orthodox model, money is neutral (at least in the long run) and cannot prevent achievement of full employment equilibrium (again, at least in the long run).

Post Keynesians, for the most part, view the cycle as a monetary phenomenon.

Money causes fluctuations and generates real effects on employment and output. In contrast, orthodoxy explains short-run deviations from equilibrium as a result of policies that temporarily fool people, such as the central bank arbitrarily increasing or reducing money growth. Otherwise, the cycle is explained as a result of shocks to real variables, such as labor productivity (as in Real Business Cycle theory). In the popular new classical approach, every point of the cycle is represented as an optimal, equilibrium position; there is never any involuntary unemployment. Thus, the Post Keynesian approach puts money center stage in its explanation of the business cycle, while orthodoxy either eliminates it entirely or relies on "exogenous money surprises" to explain the cycle.

The monetary circuit

While American Post Keynesians tend to focus on money as a stock variable, the Circuit School (led by Le Bourva in France and Graziani in Italy) sees money as a flow variable required to finance spending (Nell and Deleplace, 1996). "Circuitistes" generally begin with a bank advancing credit to a firm that wishes to expand production. They then trace the flow of money through the economy. Bank deposits finance production (money flows from firms to workers) and then consumption (money flows back from consumers to firms). At this point, firms can retire their loans. This extinguishes both the loan and the deposit, and destroys the money that had been created. The circuit approach thus adopts an endogenous money view – banks create the finance required for production and this finance is necessary for any production to take place.

Post Keynesians have adopted many aspects of the Circuit analysis. This has helped to rectify an earlier imbalance in their analysis – giving too much attention to stocks and insufficient attention to flows. Post Keynesians now generally recognize that money is important both as a stock held to reduce insecurity and as a flow of finance, and that to understand how the economy works it is necessary to trace the monetary flows that are financial counterparts to real spending and income flows.

The horizontalist approach

In contrast to the orthodox view that assumes banks are constrained by their reserves, Post Keynesians assert that banks can simply expand the money supply to meet demand. Banks are able to do this because, like other firms, they can issue liabilities in the expectation of making profits. The main difference between banks and other types of firms involves the nature of bank liabilities. Banks make loans by purchasing IOUs from borrowers; this results in a bank liability (usually a demand deposit) that shows up as an asset (money) for the borrower. Borrowers will almost immediately use the created demand deposit as a medium of exchange. That is, bank liabilities are the primary money used by non-banks. Even the government accepts some bank liabilities in payment of taxes, and it guarantees that many bank liabilities are redeemable at par against state currency.

Bank reserves are used as means of payment (inter-bank settlement) among banks and for payments made to the central bank. When people draw down deposits, this drains reserves from their bank. The bank will then have to either sell assets or borrow reserves from other banks in order to make up for its reserve deficiency. In the aggregate such activities merely shift reserves among banks. Aggregate reserve deficiencies can only be rectified by the central bank. In fact, reserve deficiencies automatically lead the central bank to lend reserves. Consequently, reserves are not discretionary in the short run; the central bank determines the price of reserves (within some constraints), but then it must provide reserves on demand to hit its "price" target (the Federal Funds Rate in the US, or the Bank Rate in the UK). Were the central bank *not* to do this, excess or deficient reserves would cause the Federal Funds Rate (or the Bank Rate) to move immediately away from its target.

This view has been called "the horizontalist approach", because the supply of bank money is determined endogenously by the demand for bank loans, rather than exogenously by government (Moore, 1988). Monetary policy operates primarily through interest rate effects; any impact it has on the quantity of money is indirect. It is the private demand for loans, plus the willingness of banks to lend, that determines the quantity of loans (and thus deposits) created. The supply of loans is never independent of demand; banks supply loans only because someone is willing to borrow bank money. One can think of the supply of bank money as horizontal at the loan rate of interest, with banks supplying loans on demand.

Another conclusion that follows from this analysis is that the interest rate cannot be determined by the supply of loans and the demand for loans, since supply and demand are not independent. Rather, banks are price setters in the loan markets; they then meet the demand for loans, with some quantity rationing, at that price.

Short-term retail interest rates can be taken as a markup over short-term wholesale interest rates, which are controlled by central bank policy. The central bank sets the overnight inter-bank rate, its main policy tool. Other short-term rates are derived by marking up the inter-bank rate. Most banks will not be able to match exactly their retail loans and deposits. Some will be able to make more retail loans than they can retain in deposits (suffering a clearing drain), while others will find fewer loan customers than depositors (resulting in a surplus reserve position). Banks then use wholesale markets to obtain reserves by issuing liabilities (large denomination certificates of deposit) or borrowing reserves from other banks, while surplus banks will lend reserves.

On this view, controlling bank reserves cannot be a discretionary policy instrument. Most bank reserves are actually supplied by the Treasury as a result of fiscal policy (spending by government). When the Treasury writes a check, this is normally deposited into the banking system, adding reserves. On the other hand, when a taxpayer writes a check to the government, this results in a debit to the reserves of the banking system as a whole. Government spending and tax receipts will never match perfectly on a day-to-day basis, even if the budget is balanced over the course of the year. This means that each day, fiscal activities by the government will cause fluctuations in bank reserves. For this reason, the central bank intervenes on a daily basis to offset any impacts from fiscal operations. The main instrument used is the purchase or sale of government bonds that will add or drain reserves, respectively. These daily interventions are necessarily defensive, which means that the central bank can not use open market operations as an offensive policy instrument. Indeed, an attempt to use open market sales or purchases in an offensive manner would cause the overnight inter-bank rate to rise or fall without limit. For this reason, all central banks accommodate private bank demands for reserves – supplying just the right amount to enable banks to hold the amount of reserves required or desired.

The Post Keynesian incomes approach to inflation

Recall that in the orthodox approach an "invisible hand" establishes equilibrium relative prices that simultaneously clear all markets. Each price reflects relative scarcity. Nominal prices, in turn, are established in terms of one commodity (a numeraire). Holding velocity constant, the aggregate price level is determined by the quantity of the money commodity, given the full employment of all other commodities.

Post Keynesians reject this formulation. First, for Post Keynesians what matters is nominal price, not relative price. Second, most prices are "administered" to accomplish a number of firm-specific goals and no priority is given to market clearing over other goals. And third, the quantity of money is endogenously determined so that the causation of the quantity equation is reversed – price times quantity determines the quantity of money required, given velocity (which Post Keynesians do not take as fixed).

The Post Keynesian approach to pricing at the microeconomic level is dealt with in Chapter 3. Hyman Minsky helped to develop the Post Keynesian approach to inflation, or the determination of prices at the macroeconomic level. For Minsky, financial commitments made are in nominal terms and all income flows are in nominal terms. It matters whether a family or a firm has a nominal inflow that is greater than its nominal outflow. Money cannot be neutral in this sort of world; and nominal prices are administered in large part to gain control over nominal inflows.

Minsky (1986: Ch. 7) argued that prices in a monetary production economy perform five main functions. They ensure (1) that a surplus is generated, (2) that some of the surplus goes to owners of capital, (3) that the market (or demand) price of capital assets is consistent with current production costs (or supply price), (4) that business debts can be repaid, and (5) that resources are directed toward the investment sector. Let us briefly examine these points.

The price of consumption goods must be high enough above wages in that sector so that some consumption goods will be left for workers in other sectors. This allows us to employ workers in the investment sector (and in the government and trade sectors). At the microlevel, each capitalist must be able to obtain a markup over labor costs. However, at the macro level, the price level determines the aggregate potential surplus to be divided among all firms in society. Capitals then compete at the microlevel for shares of aggregate profit flows.

What generates this aggregate surplus? As the Kalecki equation shows, aggregate profits equal the sum of investment plus consumption out of profits plus the government deficit and the trade surplus, less saving out of wages. In the simplest model (no government deficit, balanced trade, and no saving out of wages), profits equal investment plus capitalist consumption. If prices are set high enough so that workers cannot buy all the output, capitalists can get the rest so long as they spend on investment and consumption.

Market power and the ability to set the price is critical in determining who gets credit, but the amount of surplus available at the aggregate level depends on the aggregate markup. This, in turn, depends on capitalist spending, mainly investment (supplemented by capitalist consumption, government deficit spending, and trade surpluses in the expanded model). Market power and technological efficiency only affect the distribution of profits, but not aggregate profits. It is the aggregate spending on investment that generates the profits that validate the accumulated capital in the sense that gross profit income is required to service debt incurred to finance investment that occurred in the past.

In this sort of world there is no reason to believe that an equilibrium exists and even less reason to believe that it would be stable. Prices in the real world are nominal, and they are administered to achieve a variety of goals besides clearing markets. This is not to suggest that firms can achieve desired prices; the aggregate markup depends on aggregate spending, and if spending is too low, capitalists on average will not achieve their desired markups (in other words, actual prices realized will be below those that were desired). In this case, they may not be able to service their debt – which has negative consequences for economic stability.

As discussed above, inflation does not matter much to orthodox theory; although it might fool people in the short run, in the long run it cannot have any effect. Indeed, orthodox economists have empirically estimated that rates of inflation up to 40 percent a year have no measurable effects on GDP growth (Ahmed and Rogers, 2000; Bruno and Easterly, 1998). Nevertheless, orthodox policy prescriptions call for a vigilant central bank to watch over inflation rates. They are willing to impose very high short-run costs in the form of high unemployment and low GDP growth in order to attain low inflation even though their theory cannot explain why they should be concerned with inflation at all.

In contrast, Post Keynesians believe that nominal prices do matter. The ability to administer prices is essential given long-lived and expensive capital equipment. As Ingham (2000) notes, money prices are the result of complex power struggles – both between capital and labor, and among capitalists. When labor is strong, it can push up wages; for individual firms to earn profits, they must raise prices in compensation. This could be called "cost-push" inflation, and would likely result from decentralized wage bargaining in the presence of strong labor unions, with each individual union trying to obtain larger-than-average wage increases for its members and possibly generating a wage–price spiral. On the other hand, markup or profits inflation results when firms are able to raise their markup over wage costs. At the firm level, the markup is largely the result of oligopolistic pricing processes; however, as discussed, the aggregate markup is determined by certain kinds of spending. Thus, the aggregate markup over wage costs will be higher if investment spending, the government deficit, the trade surplus, or capitalist consumption is higher. All things equal, a society with rising investment or exports or government deficits as a percentage of GDP will face higher rates of inflation, as the aggregate markup will have to rise to ensure that domestic workers can purchase only a falling share of output. The only alternative would be for nominal wages to fall, allowing the markup to rise without forcing prices up.

In addition to incomes inflation, price increases can result from rising spot prices. The best example would be an increase in energy prices, such as those experienced during the 1970s and repeated on a lesser scale in 2000. Rising energy prices affect the cost of producing almost all goods and services. Firms will attempt to pass these along in the form of higher prices. If workers try to maintain their nominal income shares (and real wages), and if firms attempt to maintain markups, this would generate a wage–price spiral. In a monetary production economy, inflation is more benign than deflation. Inflation tends to redistribute shares toward economically powerful groups – from workers to capitalists, from non-unionized to unionized workers, from unskilled to skilled workers, from fixed income pensioners to those of working age, and from competitive sectors to oligopolistic sectors. It also tends to reduce debt burdens (and real returns to creditors). This tends to favor low-income households as well as industry over finance. On balance, the effects of inflation may encourage investment and economic growth.

In contrast, deflation not only has significant redistribution effects (opposite to those listed above), but it also increases debt burdens. This favors *rentiers* over debtors, but only if the debtors do not default. Significant deflation will generate bankruptcies, in which case even creditors are no better off. Indeed, Fisher's debt deflation theory attributes the severity of the Great Depression to price deflation that generated a snowball of bankruptcies and destroyed financial wealth. Thus, Post Keynesians generally recognize that deflation is a much more serious problem than is inflation.

Policy implications

Post Keynesians reject the orthodox approach to fighting inflation, which is to slow economic growth; and they have traditionally offered some form of incomes policy to deal with incomes inflation. Centralized wage bargaining involving workers, capitalists, and government can reduce the danger of a wage–price spiral. Such an approach has been followed in Scandinavian countries and to a lesser extent in Canada. Some Post Keynesians (Weintraub and Wallich, 1978) have formulated more formal structures, such as tax-based incomes policies, which use taxes to penalize firms that award wage increases above some established level (usually related to productivity increases). Others (Lerner and Colander, 1980) have advanced a market-based anti-inflation policy, which allows firms to buy or sell the right to raise prices.

To control spot-price inflation (such as oil price shocks), Post Keynesians have advocated using buffer stocks (Davidson, 1994). Under a buffer stock program the government buys commodities when prices are falling and sells them when prices are rising, thereby helping to stabilize prices. These programs stabilize individual prices; but if some of the commodities are an important part of the consumer basket, buffer stocks would help stabilize the overall price level. For example, stabilizing energy prices would help stabilize the price of most goods, as energy enters directly and indirectly into the production of almost everything.

Labor would be an even better buffer stock. Labor enters into the production of all goods and services; and wages are the most important cost of production. Indeed, economists have long maintained that a buffer stock of unemployed labor can help keep down wage increases and thus inflation. This idea lies behind Marx's "reserve army of the unemployed" as well as the infamous NAIRU (non-accelerating inflation rate of unemployment) and supposed Phillips curve trade-off. But keeping unemployment high in order to moderate wages has many undesirable effects. First, unemployment is costly in terms of lost output and lost income to workers and their families. Second, unemployment will not keep wage demands down if the unemployed are not good substitutes for workers who enjoy market power. If labor markets are segmented, with a primary, oligopolized sector employing highly educated workers in jobs with stable career paths, and a secondary, competitive sector offering temporary, low-skilled and lowly paid jobs to others, high unemployment may simply depress the already low wages in the secondary sector and have little impact on primary sector wages or inflation.

For these reasons, some economists have advocated using a buffer stock of employed labor, rather than unemployment, to help to stabilize wages and prices (Minsky, 1986; Harvey, 1989; Gordon, 1997; Wray, 1998).

A buffer stock program would have the government offer a job to anyone ready, willing, and able to work. The wage and benefit package would be fixed at some level, which would become the base package for the economy. The government would stand ready to "buy" and "sell" labor, offering jobs to anyone who showed up, and offering workers to any employers willing to hire workers out of the buffer stock. In boom times the government would sell labor and help dampen wage pressures; during recessions, buffer stock employment would grow and maintain wage rates, since workers could always leave the private sector and take buffer stock jobs.

Employment in the buffer stock program would be superior to

unemployment because it would prevent deterioration of labor skills, maintain income at a base level, and could actually be geared toward enhancing the education and skills of its employees to make them more productive. Of course, employers would have to offer a more attractive job, or a better wage and benefit package, to induce workers out of the buffer stock pool.

This approach is also consistent with the neo-Chartalist approach to money. Chartalism emphasizes that government is the monopoly supplier of high-powered money. As such, it can always buy anything for sale in the domestic currency. This means it can always run a buffer stock program without having to fear that it will run out of money. Thus, the labor buffer stock program would simultaneously achieve full employment of labor (which cannot otherwise be achieved in a monetary production economy) and would help to stabilize prices by dampening wage fluctuations.

References

Ahmed, S. and Rogers, J.H. (2000) "Inflation and the Great Ratios: Long-Term Evidence from the United States," *Journal of Monetary Economics*, 45: 33–5.

Bruno, M. and Easterly, W. (1998) "Inflation Crises and Long-Run Growth," *Journal of Monetary Economics*, 41: 3–26.

Brunner, K. (1968) "The Role of Money and Monetary Policy," *Federal Reserve Bank of St. Louis Review*, 50: 9–24.

Dalziel, P. (1996) "The Keynesian Multiplier, Liquidity Preference and Endogenous Money," *Journal of Post Keynesian Economics*, 18: 311–31.

Davidson, P. (1978) *Money and the Real World*, London: Macmillan.

Davidson, P. (1994) *Post Keynesian Monetary Theory*, Aldershot: Edward Elgar.

Dow, A. and Dow, S. (1989) "Endogenous Money Creation and Idle Balances," in J. Pheby (ed.) *New Directions in Post Keynesian Economics*, Aldershot: Edward Elgar, pp. 147–64.

Gordon, W. (1997) "Job Assurance–the Job Guarantee Revisited," *Journal of Economic Issues*, 31: 826–34.

Hahn, F. (1983) *Money and Inflation*, Cambridge, MA: MIT Press.

Harvey, P. (1989) *Securing the Right to Employment*, Princeton: Princeton University Press.

Ingham, G. (2000) "'Babylonian Madness': On the Historical and Sociological Origins of Money," in J. Smithin (ed.) *What is Money?* London and New York: Routledge, pp. 16–41.

Keynes, J.M. (1964) [1936] *The General Theory of Employment Interest and Money*, New York: Harcourt Brace.

Keynes, J.M. (1973) *The General Theory and After: Part II Defence and Development, The Collected Writings of John Maynard Keynes*, vol. XIV, London: Macmillan.

Keynes, J.M. (1976) [1930] *A Treatise on Money*, vol. 1. *The Pure Theory of Money*, New York: Harcourt Brace.

Keynes, J.M. (1982) *Social, Political and Literary Writings, The Collected Writings of John Maynard Keynes*, vol. XXVIII, London: Macmillan.

Knapp, G.F. [1924] (1973) *The State Theory of Money*, Clifton, NJ: Augustus M. Kelley.

Lerner, A.P. (1947) "Money as a Creature of the State," *American Economic Review*, 37: 312–17.

Lerner, A.P. and Colander, D. (1980) *MAP: A Market Anti-Inflation Plan*, New York: Harcourt Brace Jovanovich.

Minsky, H.P. (1986) *Stabilizing an Unstable Economy*, New Haven: Yale University Press.

Moore, B. (1978) "Monetary Factors," in A.S. Eichner (ed.) *A Guide to Post Keynesian Economics*, Armonk, NY: M.E. Sharpe, pp. 120–38.

Moore, B. (1988) *Horizontalists and Verticalists: The Macroeconomics of Credit Money*, Cambridge: Cambridge University Press.

Nell, E. and Deleplace, G. (1996) *Money in Motion: The Post-Keynesian and Circulation Approaches*, London: Macmillan.

Papadimitriou, D. and Wray, L.R. (1994) "Flying Blind: The Federal Reserve's Experiment with Unobservables," *Public Policy Brief* no. 15, Jerome Levy Economics Institute.

Robinson, J. (1979) *The Generalisation of the General Theory and other Essays*, New York: St. Martin's Press.

Schumpeter, J.A. (1954) *History of Economic Analysis*, New York: Oxford University Press.

Weintraub, S. and Wallich, H. (1978) "A Tax-Based Incomes Policy," in S. Weintraub (ed.) *Keynes, Keynesians and Monetarists*, Philadelphia: University of Pennsylvania Press, pp. 259–80.

Wray, L.R. (1990) *Money and Credit in Capitalist Economies: The Endogenous Money Approach*, Aldershot: Edward Elgar.

Wray, L.R. (1998) *Understanding Modern Money: The Key to Full Employment and Price Stability*, Cheltenham: Edward Elgar.

9 Macrodynamics

Mark Setterfield

Introduction

Macrodynamic theory studies how macroeconomic variables such as total output, employment, and the general price level change over time. Within this broad definition, it is useful to distinguish between price dynamics and quantity dynamics. Price dynamics is concerned with rising prices and theories of inflation. This chapter focuses on quantity dynamics, or the branch of economics concerned with the growth and development of economies over time.

In the *Guide to Post Keynesian Economics*, Cornwall (1978) presents neoclassical and Post Keynesian macrodynamics as a study in contrast. According to Cornwall, Post Keynesian macrodynamics studies qualitative and structural change as economies grow and develop, while the neoclassical approach sees growth as a steady, balanced process. Moreover, while investment is central to Post Keynesian analysis, providing sources of both demand and new productive capacity, accumulation does not affect growth in the neoclassical theory. Finally, Post Keynesian macrodynamics is shown to be rich with possibilities for policy interventions, while its neoclassical counterpart is bereft of policy implications.

In the years immediately following publication of the *Guide*, neoclassical economists developed a renewed interest in growth theory and macrodynamics (see Romer, 1986; Lucas, 1988). Fine (1997, 2000) argues that this forms part of a neoclassical "colonizing project," which aims to show how results previously associated with heterodox economics can arise within the standard neoclassical framework of individual optimization subject to constraints.

But whatever caused the neoclassical revival in growth theory, the consequences of this revival affect several of the points made by Cornwall (1978). In particular, some of what Cornwall describes as unique features of Post Keynesian macrodynamics can now be found in neoclassical macrodynamic models. However, despite the greater overlap that exists today, any similarities between neoclassical and Post Keynesian macrodynamics remain superficial. Beneath the surface lie marked differences between the visions of growth in Post Keynesian and neoclassical economics. These create substantive differences in the models that Post Keynesian and neoclassical economists use to describe macrodynamics.

Harrod and the genesis of modern macrodynamics

Modern macrodynamics can be traced to the pioneering work of Harrod (1939; also see Domar, 1946). Harrod points to the dual role of investment in an expanding economy. Investment serves as both a source of aggregate demand (in typical Keynesian fashion) and a source of additional productive capacity (and hence aggregate supply). Recognizing that investment has both demand and supply-side effects, Harrod raised two questions about the actual level of investment in an economy. First, will the demand and supply effects of investment be reconciled? That is, will the aggregate demand that investment spending generates (through the multiplier) justify the new productive capacity it creates, by ensuring the full utilization of this capacity? Second, will the resulting economic expansion be consistent with the full employment of an expanding labor force?

For Harrod, nothing guarantees that the actual and natural (i.e. full employment) rates of growth will be equal. There is no variable that can adjust in order to give us automatic full employment. Moreover, any lack of effective demand at the macroeconomic level that leaves capital under-utilized will lead to adjustments that broaden the discrepancy between aggregate supply and demand (or between the actual and warranted rates of growth). This is a vision in which demand, dominated by volatile investment decisions that are subject to uncertainty, governs macrodynamics. As a result, economic expansion is inherently unstable: growth will always be uneven and subject to fluctuations. At the same time, full employment will not automatically be achieved.

Responses to Harrod: demand versus supply-side visions of growth

The work of Harrod provoked two different responses. Post Keynesians drew attention to the interaction of demand and supply. The claim that "demand matters" in the determination of growth outcomes became a hallmark of Post Keynesian macrodynamics. This is true whether we conceive Post Keynesian macrodynamics narrowly, as consisting of Kalecki–Robinson (see Lavoie, 1992: Ch. 6) and Kaldorian models (McCombie and Thirlwall, 1994), or more expansively, to include theories of transformational growth (see Nell, 1992) and traverse analysis (see Halevi and Kriesler, 1992).

The neoclassical response, meanwhile, conceived growth and development as a supply-side process. The first generation of neoclassical models, based on the work of Solow (1956), focused on the substitution of capital for labor, and the ability of the economy to vary the capital–labor ratio until the actual, warranted and natural rates of growth are reconciled.[1] This "solution" to Harrod's growth problems, however, requires that saving creates investment. But the autonomy of investment from savings is a key macroeconomic fact according to Post Keynesian economists. By denying this autonomy, the Solow model allows any expansion of potential output on the supply side to translate automatically into an expansion of actual output. There can be no effective demand failures because aggregate demand adjusts automatically to accommodate aggregate supply.[2]

This supply-side vision of growth and development also characterizes the second generation of neoclassical models – the so-called neoclassical endogenous growth (NEG) theories. These theories revise the technical relationship between inputs and outputs in the Solow production function. Specifically, capital inputs (defined broadly to include human and physical capital and technical know-how) are subject to non-diminishing marginal returns, so that their continuous accumulation contributes to long-run growth.[3] So while the long-run growth rate is exogenous in the Solow model, the supply-side source of growth (the accumulation of capital inputs) is explained within NEG theory, although usually in terms of other exogenous, supply-side variables.[4]

Influenced by New Keynesian theories of the impact of demand on real variables in the presence of price rigidities, some NEG models allow demand to affect the rate of growth. However, in all these models, price reductions will automatically increase aggregate demand, thereby allowing increases in supply to create their own demand. So, although variations in demand can influence growth in some NEG models, they are a peripheral influence. Growth episodes are usually analyzed solely in terms of the supply side in NEG theory, since supply can create its own demand.

This contrasts sharply with the Post Keynesian treatment of demand, which begins with the separation of investment and savings decisions. Expectations regarding investment are subject to fundamental uncertainty and no variable can coordinate investment decisions with prior changes in aggregate saving behavior. As a result, for Post Keynesians, there is some autonomy of aggregate demand from aggregate supply conditions in the determination of output; increases in supply do not automatically create their own demand, so the supply side cannot be the sole focus of growth analysis.

In sum, aggregate demand is thought of in fundamentally different ways in neoclassical and Post Keynesian macroeconomics. Demand factors are essential in Post Keynesian macrodynamics. In neoclassical theory, however, demand does not typically influence growth; instead, Say's Law is alive and well.

The characteristics of demand-led growth

Demand stands front and center in Post Keynesian discussions of growth and development for two reasons. First, aggregate demand influences the utilization of productive resources at any point in time. We cannot assume that there will be sufficient demand to justify the productive capacity that firms have created, or to fully employ the labor force. A growing economy may therefore experience discrepancies between its actual and potential expansions of output. Lengthy episodes of high unemployment in the history of capitalism indicate that this is not just a theoretical possibility, but also a description of how real economies operate.

Second, the expansion of demand may affect the development of productive resources over time. This is not just because, as Harrod noted, decisions to invest create both additional aggregate demand and new productive capacity, but also because the growth of demand influences the size of the labor force and the pace of technological progress.[5] Labor force participation rates, the number of hours worked and the geographical migration of labor are all sensitive to the expansion of demand (Cornwall, 1977). Meanwhile, the willingness to adopt new technology, to reorganize the production process in order to increase specialization, and to engage in research and development, are all encouraged by the effects of demand growth on firms' sales and revenue expectations (see Boyer and Petit, 1991). Demand-induced labor force growth and technological progress, the latter giving rise to dynamic increasing returns to scale, means that both the full employment expansion path of the economy (Harrod's natural rate of growth) and the economy's proximity to this expansion path are influenced by demand.

It should be clear that in Post Keynesian macrodynamics growth is both endogenous (determined by forces operating within the economy) and path dependent, since there is no growth trajectory acting as a "center of gravity" towards which the economy is inexorably and inevitably drawn. Rather than being predefined, long-run growth and development depend on a succession of short- and medium-term developments along a historical adjustment path. As we move along this path, changes in demand affect both the utilization of productive resources and the development of these productive resources over time. For Post Keynesians, then, potential and actual growth both depend on the extent to which the economy has grown in the past. In part, this is because of the induced supply-side effects of demand-led growth on productive capacity as described above. But path dependence also arises because of the expectational nature of the components of aggregate demand itself. When expectations are subject to fundamental uncertainty about the future, they are influenced (in a non-deterministic manner) by the growth of demand in the recent past, and the extent to which short-run expectations have been realized or disappointed (see Setterfield, 1999).

These characteristics of Post Keynesian macrodynamics lead to some fundamental contrasts with neoclassical macrodynamics. The Solow model, for example, suggests that growth is governed by a path-independent, long-run equilibrium defined in terms of exogenous data. The contrasts with NEG theory are more subtle but no less striking. Growth is endogenous in an NEG model, since it emerges from the equilibrium solution of the model itself (unlike Solow's theory, in which the economy's growth rate is datum). But this is a minimal conception of endogenous growth, because the equilibrium growth rate in NEG models is still defined in terms of unexplained, exogenous data.[6] NEG theory only pushes back the boundaries of exogeneity, explaining what was previously taken as given in terms of new exogenous variables (Fine, 2000).

A more expansive conception of endogenous growth is found in Post Keynesian macrodynamics. For Post Keynesians, the growth and development processes are endogenous in the sense of being determined by their own past history. In this analysis, "the only truly exogenous factor is whatever exists at a moment of time, as a heritage of the past" (Kaldor, 1985: 61). Path dependence is, therefore, essential to the Post Keynesian conception of endogenous growth, something that cannot be said of NEG theory.

Some NEG models allow for multiple growth equilibria, with the result that both initial conditions and subsequent shocks can affect the precise equilibrium growth rate that the economy achieves. These models are then claimed to demonstrate path-dependent growth. However, multiple equilibria are not a necessary feature of NEG models. More importantly, there is far more to the claim that "history matters" than the idea that initial conditions or shocks matter. In Post Keynesian macrodynamics, economic adjustments do more than just select among pre-defined long-run outcomes – they help to determine the very nature of these outcomes. New growth paths arise as economic expansion induces transformative structural changes in consumer preferences, technologies, and social institutions. The economy effectively creates its own future in the course of its growth and development. Furthermore, the structural changes associated with this process involve novelty. In other words, they cannot be fully anticipated by decision-makers in the economy, creating fundamental uncertainty about the future. This more expansive conception of path dependency, which forms the heart of Post Keynesian macrodynamics, is anathema to neoclassical economics.[7]

Other prominent features of Post Keynesian macrodynamics

From the discussion up to this point, it is easy to identify two further features of Post Keynesian macrodynamics. First, the lack of a long-run equilibrium in Post Keynesian macrodynamics, its non-deterministic description of path-dependent growth outcomes, and the volatility of investment all suggest that growth and development are intrinsically uneven processes. Economies are likely to experience fluctuations in their growth rates over time. Moreover, these fluctuations can affect an economy's long-run (trend) rate of growth as a result of path dependency.

Some Post Keynesians go further than this, arguing that growth is not just uneven but also unbalanced. For example, growth changes the pattern of consumer demand and hence the types of goods that an economy produces, causing factor inputs and outputs to grow in different proportions in different sectors of the economy (Cornwall, 1977; Pasinetti, 1981). This creates structural or compositional changes in economic activity, such as changes in the distribution of employment between industries, that can affect the growth process itself (see Cornwall, 1972; 1977; Setterfield, 1997). Uneven and unbalanced growth, however, are peripheral to neoclassical macrodynamics. Neoclassical economics, by analyzing macrodynamics in terms of stable, steady-state growth rates, typically precludes the possibility of unbalanced growth and reduces fluctuations to exogenous shocks that have no impact on long-run growth.

A second, salient feature of Post Keynesian macrodynamics is its emphasis on accumulating and utilizing productive resources, rather than their scarcity and allocation. For Post Keynesians resources are not typically scarce. On the contrary, there is no guarantee that aggregate demand will be sufficient at any point in time to enable an economy to reach its potential output; and there is no automatic tendency for such an outcome to be reached over time. Furthermore, since investment is a key component of aggregate demand and is instrumental in determining the economy's realized growth rate, and since the potential or natural rate of growth depends on technological progress embodied in specific, tangible assets, it is natural for Post Keynesians to emphasize the role of accumulation in the growth process.

In contrast, neoclassical macrodynamics assumes that demand adjusts automatically to accommodate expansions of aggregate supply. As a result, concern with the utilization of available productive resources disappears. It is an explicit feature of the Solow model that accumulation is irrelevant for long-run growth; savings (and hence investment) can only affect the level and not the rate of growth of per capita income. NEG theory has rectified this problem, allowing neoclassical growth theory to connect growth to the rate at which factor inputs are accumulated. However, these rates of accumulation typically depend on the allocation of scarce resources. Although it is the proximate source of growth, then, accumulation is, in fact, reduced to a problem of resource allocation. Furthermore, the inputs accumulated in NEG models are usually malleable or "putty like," so that they can always be made compatible with existing productive assets. Problems arising from the incompatibility of heterogeneous assets embodying different technical standards, while recognized in Post Keynesian macrodynamics, are absent from neoclassical theory. Neoclassical analysis, to make the point again, is carried out in "logical time." It tends to portray economic activity as happening all at once. In contrast, Post Keynesian economics recognizes the sequential and historical structure of time, where past events influence current outcomes.

Avenues for further research

Some aspects of Post Keynesian macrodynamics remain relatively underdeveloped and should attract greater attention in the near future. One such aspect is the financing of investment and hence growth. Certainly, it would be unfair to overlook the role of savings (specifically, corporate savings or retained earnings) as a source of finance in Kalecki–Robinson growth models. In these models, an important link between pricing, investment, and growth emerges. Firms set prices, embodying markups over average costs, that are designed to generate sufficient retained earnings to fund planned investment. However, Post Keynesian macrodynamics has thus far paid little attention to the role of endogenous credit money as a source of investment financing in the context of growth models. In capitalist monetary–production economies, money is important thanks to its unique liquidity characteristics and its role as a source of finance in an environment where economic activities are separated in historical time. An obvious starting point for the development of a Post Keynesian monetary macrodynamics is the theory of endogenous credit money (see Chapter 8).

A second underdeveloped aspect of Post Keynesian macrodynamics concerns the role of institutions (such as norms, conventions, and rules) in the growth process. Institutions matter for neoclassical economists, because they lower transaction costs and improve the efficiency of resource allocation. For example, organized capital markets improve the interaction between lenders and borrowers. Because resource allocation is fundamental to accumulation and growth in NEG theory, this allows neoclassical economists to connect institutions with the growth process.

While recognizing that improved exchange relations may contribute to growth and development, Post Keynesians regard this understanding of institutions as too narrow. First, because Post Keynesians view the future as uncertain and because uncertainty precludes the possibility of dynamic optimization, institutions are seen as an invaluable basis for action. Norms and conventions provide grounds for engaging in specific levels and types of investment spending, even when the "optimal" level or type of investment is impossible to calculate. Moreover, by indicating the likely future behavior of others, institutions provide important information to decision-makers, who must form expectations and then act in an uncertain world.

Second, Post Keynesians see individuals as interdependent, social beings rather than the isolated "atoms" of neoclassical theory. This gives rise to concerns with issues of distribution and equity. For Post Keynesians, the economy is characterized by socioeconomic conflict over issues such as relative factor rewards and control over the production process. Institutions can play an important role in abating this distributional conflict. Indeed, socioeconomic conflict and institutional solutions to this conflict are central to contemporary Post Keynesian theories of inflation (see Chapter 8).

Distributional conflict featured prominently in one of the earliest contributions to Post Keynesian macrodynamic analysis (Kaldor, 1955/6). And changes in the distribution of income and their impact on growth are a major theme in modern Kaleckian growth models (see Blecker, 2001). Some recent analyses have even suggested that institutional solutions to distributional conflict can affect accumulation, technical change and the composition of output, and hence the rate of growth (Setterfield, 1997; Cassetti, 2001). But the role of institutions in mediating conflict remains relatively undeveloped in Post Keynesian macroeconomics, especially when compared with its treatment in the Regulation School (see Boyer, 1990) and the Social Structures of Accumulation approach (see Kotz *et al.*, 1994).

Policy implications

What are the policy implications of Post Keynesian macrodynamics? As mentioned earlier, Cornwall (1978) argues that the first generation of neoclassical macrodynamics is void of policy implications. This is because the Solow model describes the economy as following a unique and steady growth path determined by factors exogenous to the economy. More recently, NEG theory has re-examined the roles of capital accumulation and technical progress in economic growth. This has generated numerous policy proposals, such as lower investment taxes and government subsidies for investment as well as for research and development, which are designed to help expand the supplies of capital and technical know-how and increase the growth rate. In general, having connected the economics of scarce resource allocation to the processes of accumulation and growth, NEG theorists can now apply policy proposals from welfare and public economics, where they affect the level of per capita income, to the field of macrodynamics, where they affect the growth of per capita income (Fine, 2000). But these policy proposals differ markedly from Post Keynesian policy recommendations.

First, neoclassical policies focus on the supply side. But in Post Keynesian macrodynamics, growth is demand led. Post Keynesians emphasize the role of monetary and fiscal policies that affect the expansion and volatility of demand in determining both the realized and potential rates of growth.

Second, the path-dependent world of uneven growth and development in Post Keynesian macrodynamics is characterized by uncertainty about the future. This makes room for the Schumpeterian entrepreneur, whose role is to act decisively (even in the face of uncertainty), when reasonable decisions may have been made differently. The Schumpeterian entrepreneur is absent from neoclassical macrodynamics because there can be no discretionary responses in a neoclassical world. Rather, the known and structurally stable economic environment calls for a passive, coordinating role by the neoclassical decision maker, whose optimal choices are products of the structurally predetermined neoclassical economy.

The distinction between discretion and meaningful choice on the one hand, and passive coordination of extraneous forces on the other, carries over into the public policy arena. Hence, the policy recommendations of NEG theory posit the same passive, coordinating role for policy-makers that they posit for private decision-makers. Both sets of agents see the economic environment as external, and its structure fixed independently of any decisions made within it.

In contrast, the openness of the Post Keynesian economic environment, and the capacity for discretion and creative action, means that policy-makers can always make different, reasonable decisions. They are capable of acting in ways that will shape and create the economic future, for better or for worse.[9] This capacity for policy intervention in Post Keynesian macrodynamics is accompanied by a clear rationale for such intervention. Given the unevenness of the growth process and the influence of the realized growth path on the use and development an economy's productive resources, state intervention can improve economic performance and enhance the prospects for long-run growth. None of this is to say that policy intervention *will* be effectively implemented by public bodies. Such judgment presupposes a theory of the state, which is beyond the confines of this chapter (but see Chapter 10). Nevertheless, within Post Keynesian macrodynamics, it is possible to envisage an entrepreneurial or developmental state, the likes of which cannot be conceived in neoclassical theory.[10]

Notes

1   The long-run rate of growth in the Solow model is, therefore, the natural rate of growth, which is taken as exogenously given.
2   As such, there can be no inequality of the actual, warranted, and natural rates of growth in the Solow model in the long run. Since full employment savings automatically create an equivalent flow of investment spending, labor supply conditions are (for any given state of technology) the only constraint on the level of economic activity at any point in time. Labor resources cannot be underutilized if the economy automatically generates sufficient investment to offset the full employment level of savings. This precludes any systematic departure of the actual from the natural rate of growth. Meanwhile, if any additional saving necessarily creates an offsetting flow of investment spending, there is no room for the independent variations in investment spending due to disappointed demand expectations that are associated with the dynamics of Harrod's warranted rate. This is because there are no disappointed demand expectations!
3   This is not true of the Solow model, in which diminishing returns to capital preclude long-run growth based on accumulation.
4   Examples of these exogenous variables include the rate of time preference and the preferences of workers that affect their decisions to accumulate human capital.
5   It can also affect the transfer of resources between sectors of the economy with different growth potentials in an environment of unbalanced growth (see Cornwall, 1972, 1977).
6   The reader is referred back to footnote 4 for examples of this exogenous data.
7   Because structural change can be initiated by ordinary adjustments within the economy and does not require the intervention of "shocks", and because such change involves novelty, Post Keynesian macrodynamics can actually be described as *evolutionary* rather than just path dependent (see Cornwall and Cornwall, 2001: Ch. 6).
8   As we have already noted, in NEG models with multiple equilibria, fluctuations caused by exogenous shocks *can* affect the long-run growth rate. However, it is interesting to note that only recently, a group of prominent neoclassical macroeconomists concluded that the idea that long-run real outcomes are independent of short-run disturbances is sufficiently consensual to be regarded as part of a teachable "core" of neoclassical macroeconomic theory (see the contributions by Solow, Taylor, Eichenbaum, Blinder, and Blanchard to the *American Economic Review*, 87: 230–46).
9   See Whalen (1998) on the "creative state."
10   I am grateful to John Cornwall and Steve Pressman for comments on an earlier draft of this paper.

References

Blecker, R. (2001) "Distribution, Demand and Growth in Neo-Kaleckian Macro Models," in M. Setterfield (ed.) *The Economics of Demand-Led Growth: Challenging the Supply Side Vision of the Long Run*, Cheltenham: Edward Elgar.

Boyer, R. (1990) *The Regulation School: A Critical Introduction*, New York: Columbia University Press.

Boyer, R. and Petit, P. (1991) "Kaldor's Growth Theories: Past, Present and Prospects for the Future," in E.J. Nell and W. Semmler (eds.) *Nicholas Kaldor and Mainstream Economics: Confrontation or Convergence?* London, Macmillan, pp. 485–517.

Cassetti, M. (2001) "Conflict, Inflation, Distribution and Terms of Trade in the Kaleckian Model," in M. Setterfield (ed.) *The Economics of Demand-Led Growth: Challenging the Supply Side Vision of the Long Run*, Cheltenham: Edward Elgar.

Cornwall, J. (1972) *Growth and Stability in a Mature Economy*, London: Martin Robertson.

Cornwall, J. (1977) *Modern Capitalism: Its Growth and Transformation*, London: Martin Robertson.

Cornwall, J. (1978) "Macrodynamics," in A. Eichner (ed.) *A Guide to Post Keynesian Economics*, Armonk, NY: M.E. Sharpe, pp. 19–33.

Cornwall, J. and Cornwall, W. (2001) *Capitalist Development in the Twentieth Century: An Evolutionary–Keynesian Analysis*, Cambridge: Cambridge University Press.

Domar, E. (1946) "Capital Expansion, Rate of Growth and Employment," *Econometrica*, 14: 137–47.

Fine, B. (1997) "The New Revolution in Economics," *Capital and Class*, 61: 143–8.

Fine, B. (2000) "Endogenous Growth Theory: A Critical Assessment," *Cambridge Journal of Economics*, 24: 245–65.

Halevi, J. and Kriesler, P. (1992) "An Introduction to the Traverse in Economic Theory," in J. Halevi, D. Laibman and E.J. Nell (eds.) *Beyond the Steady State: A Revival of Growth Theory*, New York: St. Martin's Press, pp. 225–34.

Harrod, R.F. (1939) "An Essay in Dynamic Theory," *Economic Journal*, 49: 14–33.

Kaldor, N. (1955/56) "Alternative Theories of Distribution," *Review of Economic Studies*, 23: 83–100.

Kaldor, N. (1985) *Economics Without Equilibrium*, Cardiff: University College Cardiff Press.

Kotz, D.M., McDonough, T. and Reich, M. (eds.) (1994) *Social Structures of Accumulation: The Political Economy of Growth and Crisis*, Cambridge: Cambridge University Press.

Lavoie, M. (1992) *Foundations of Post Keynesian Economic Analysis*, Aldershot: Edward Elgar.

Lucas, R. (1988) "On the Mechanics of Economic Development," *Journal of Monetary Economics*, 22: 3–42.

McCombie, J.S.L. and Thirlwall, A.P. (1994) *Economic Growth and the Balance of Payments Constraint*, London: Macmillan.

Nell, E.J. (1992) *Transformational Growth and Effective Demand: Economics After the Capital Critique*, London: Macmillan.

Pasinetti, L.L. (1981) *Structural Change and Economic Growth: A Theoretical Essay on the Dynamics of the Wealth of Nations*, Cambridge: Cambridge University Press.

Romer, P. (1986) "Increasing Returns and Long Run Growth," *Journal of Political Economy*, 94: 1002–37.

Setterfield, M.A. (1997) *Rapid Growth and Relative Decline: Modelling Macroeconomic Dynamics with Hysteresis*, London: Macmillan.

Setterfield, M.A. (1999) "Expectations, Path Dependence and Effective Demand: a Macroeconomic Model Along Keynesian Lines," *Journal of Post Keynesian Economics*, 21: 479–501.

Solow, R.M. (1956) "A Contribution to the Theory of Economic Growth," *Quarterly Journal of Economics*, 70: 65–94.

Whalen, C. (1998) "Post Keynesian Economics and the Creative State," Cornell University, mimeo.

10 The role of the state and the state budget

Steven Pressman

Introduction

The first *Guide to Post Keynesian Economics* (Eichner, 1978) contained no chapter on the state. Although the book came out in 1978, it was conceived and written several years earlier, when optimism still prevailed about using state policy to improve economic performance.

In the mid-1970s, Keynesian macroeconomics dominated the profession and developed economies performed extremely well. On every important measure of economic performance – unemployment, inflation, productivity growth, and rising living standards – the 1960s and early 1970s were a Golden Age of capitalism. Economic life was getting better and Keynesian economics was thought to be responsible for this (see Cornwall, 1994).

Things then started to turn bad. Inflation and unemployment increased at the same time in most developed countries. Productivity growth stagnated and living standards improved very little. In addition, rising budget deficits became an increasing concern. For the Group of Seven (G7) nations, average (unweighted) budget deficits soared from 1 percent of GDP between 1959 and 1970 to 3.6 percent of GDP from 1971 to 1981, and then to 4.4 percent of GDP from 1982 to 1993.

Stagflation called into question the theoretical basis of Keynesian economics and massive budget deficits led economists to question the Keynesian view that government policy should be used to remedy the problems of capitalism. This opened the door to critiques of the Keynesian view of the state and alternative views regarding the economic role of government. Two alternative viewpoints became particularly prominent. The public choice revolution, stemming from the work of Buchanan, questioned the motivations of economic policy-makers, while the Lucas Critique questioned the fundamental assumptions of Keynesian macroeconomic models. As Keynes dropped out of favor in the 1980s and the 1990s, so did his policy prescriptions to improve economic performance.

This chapter proceeds as follows. The next two sections summarize the neoclassical view and the traditional Keynesian view of the state. This will be followed by a section summarizing the main critiques of Keynes and why economists came to hold that fiscal policy was ineffective in remedying macroeconomic problems. The Post Keynesian response to these critiques and the Post Keynesian view of the state will then be set forth. The chapter concludes with a discussion of the policy implications of a Post Keynesian theory of the state.

The neoclassical view of the state

Neoclassical economists generally favor a minimal role for the state. Market economies are seen as efficient and are thought to lead to the greatest possible good for its citizens; any country that allows the market to flourish unhindered will grow and prosper. This conclusion follows logically from the most basic principle of neoclassical theory – non-coercive trade must benefit all parties involved, since parties will only take part in trade if they gain from it.

Going even further, many economists see state involvement in economic affairs as reducing individual freedom (Friedman, 1962) and leading down a road to serfdom (Hayek, 1944). Consequently, they generally support *laissez-faire* policy prescriptions.

This does not mean, however, that they reject any role for the state. The state must guarantee property rights and must enforce appropriate rules of conduct. Without such a night watchman, economic activity would not take place since successful entrepreneurs would be left at the mercy of unscrupulous thieves. Most neoclassical economists also accept three further reasons for state intervention into economic affairs.

First, government action is justified to reduce the monopoly power of individual firms or to prevent firms from acquiring monopoly power. According to neoclassical theory, trade is beneficial only if it is non-coercive. Firms with market power can extort high prices from consumers, or force workers to accept low pay and dangerous working conditions. Consequently, government must ensure that firms do not acquire such power.

Second, government action is warranted in cases with important externalities or spillover effects. When individuals gain or lose, while not taking part in a market transaction, we no longer get the best possible result from free trade. For example, if some production costs can be imposed on third parties via air and water pollution, these goods will sell below their true cost and too many goods will get produced that destroy our environment. On the other hand, too few goods get produced (like public transportation) because producers cannot charge those who benefit from reduced congestion (the people driving to work). In these cases, government must internalize the negative externality (make the polluting firm pay to clean up the environment) or provide the desired goods that firms will *not* produce because they cannot charge everyone who benefits from it.

Finally, government action is warranted when consumers cannot obtain adequate information about goods and services. If consumers cannot understand the most recent medical advances, they can easily become the dupes of someone claiming medical expertise. This is especially so in times of medical emergencies, when desperate individuals seek any possible cure for a life-threatening illness. As a result, the state needs to ensure both that medical practitioners are sanctioned by professional experts and that medical treatments are safe before they become widely available.

Keynes and the role of the state

In contrast to the neoclassical view, Keynes saw the state as an integral part of economic activity and a positive force that could be used to improve overall economic performance.

The main accomplishment of Keynes ([1936] 1964) was that he gave the state primary responsibility for overall macroeconomic performance. He did this by rejecting the view of a self-adjusting economy that could find full employment equilibrium at low rates of inflation. Instead, Keynes explained how and why an economy could remain permanently stuck at high levels of unemployment, and why it might experience high inflation or other macroeconomic problems that would continue unabated without any action on the part of the state.

Going even further, Keynes argued that the state must employ economic policies to help mitigate these economic problems. In times of high unemployment, deficit spending would be required to expand aggregate demand and put people back to work. This required some sort of tax cut and/ or increase in government expenditures. In times of high inflation, tax increases and spending cuts would be needed to reduce those expenditures that led to upward pressure on prices. Or, alternatively, some form of incomes policy would be necessary (see Chapter 8).

This view of the role of the state has important implications regarding the state budget and the national debt. In times of depression or recession, government tax collections inevitably decline as national income falls and as government spending increases for social programs such as unemployment insurance. This leads to a cyclical budget deficit – government spending exceeding taxes because the economy is at the low point of its business cycle.

Any attempt to lessen this deficit by increasing taxes or reducing government spending, Keynes argued, would make the recession worse by reducing demand for goods and these business sales. Instead, he advocated greater government spending and/or tax cuts – adding a structural budget deficit to the cyclical deficit. This would stimulate spending and help end the recession.

To improve economic performance, it did not really matter how the state spent its money; all that mattered was that the money got spent. But Keynes did have strong preferences about what the state should purchase. In a much-quoted passage, he writes about the need for more houses, hospitals, schools, and roads. But he notes that many people are likely to object to such "wasteful" government expenditures. Another approach was therefore necessary. "If the Treasury were to fill old bottles with banknotes, bury them at suitable depths

in disused coal mines which are then filled up to the surface with town rubbish
... private enterprise [would] dig the notes up and there need be no more
unemployment" (Keynes, 1964: 129).

And in a much-maligned passage, Keynes (1964: 378) called for "a somewhat
comprehensive socialization of investment". While many have taken Keynes
to be advocating government control of all business investment decisions, what
Keynes really advanced was government spending policies to stabilize the
aggregate level of investment in the national economy. When private investment
was low, he wanted the government to borrow money and engage in public
investments such as building new roads and bridges and spending more money
on schools and better education. In contrast, when business investment was
high because of great optimism, the government should stop borrowing and
cut back on its public investment. On this view, the state became responsible
for fine-tuning the economy – increasing investment spending when
unemployment was high and reducing spending when unemployment was low
and when inflation threatened.

Two critiques of the Keynesian view of the state

This Keynesian view of the state came under attack in the 1970s and the
1980s. The public choice and rational expectations revolutions questioned some
of the fundamental assumptions that Keynes made about government policy-
making. At the same time, poor economic performance caused economists to
search for a new understanding of macroeconomic problems and how they
could be mitigated.

A first problem concerns the motivations of policy-makers. Public choice
economists pointed out that there was a logical gap between the incentives
economic policy-makers face and the economic policies that they need to put
into effect.

Buchanan (and Wagner, 1977) contends that Keynesian economics depends
on the assumption that policy-makers will act in the public interest rather
than in their own self-interest. However, he points out, policy-makers are human
too, and they have human motives, desires, and capacities. If policy-makers
were rational and self-interested, they would pass legislation and develop policies
that benefit themselves; this would *not* likely lead to improved economic
performance for the whole nation. Macroeconomic policy will therefore fail to
improve economic performance and might even make things worse.

In addition, Buchanan notes that people attracted to government service
generally prefer a large role for government and are interested in improving
social well-being. This will require large budgets. Politicians also need to be
re-elected periodically. Large budgets enable them to pass out the largesse that
improves their chances of re-election. And unelected public employees will
recommend and propose large budgets, since this gives them more people to
supervise and greater incomes. These incentives create a bias towards big
government, large budgets, and deficits.

Buchanan (1958; Buchanan and Wagner, 1977) argued forcefully against government deficits, contending that public debt has many negative effects. When the government sells bonds to finance its debt, it competes with private sellers of debt and pushes up the cost of borrowing (interest rates). As a result, private investment declines. In the long run, problems are even greater. A rising debt, with rising interest burdens, increases the likelihood of a government default. Furthermore, Buchanan argued that future generations suffer from the deficit because they will have to pay higher taxes to repay the debt.

Overall, Buchanan *et al.* (1978) see Keynesian economics "as a disease that over the long run can prove fatal for the survival of democracy." It loosens the moral restraint on politicians to act in morally acceptable fashion, and it leads to the false belief that since we owe the money to ourselves there is nothing wrong with running state deficits.

Rational expectations takes a slightly different approach in its critique of Keynesian economics. Lucas (1976; Lucas and Sargent, 1978) criticized the Keynesian assumption that all macroeconomic relationships would remain unchanged in the face of policy changes enacted by policy-makers. Rational individuals who seek to maximize their own well-being, he reasoned, should change their behavior in the face of changing economic policy.

Macroeconomic models used to evaluate the consequences of different economic policies all assume that macroeconomic relationships will remain the same in the face of any policy change. But this will not be true, Lucas (and Sargent, 1978: 52) contends, because "a change in policy necessarily alters some of the structural parameters ... in a highly complex fashion." Without knowing which economic relationships change, and how they change, an econometric model is of no value in assessing alternative policies. This factor, according to Lucas, renders Keynesian macroeconomic policies ineffective.

Consider expansionary policies to lower unemployment. When policy-makers attempt to expand the economy and create jobs, Lucas argues, they will generate expectations of higher inflation among rational economic agents. But workers will not want to work more if their real wages fall, and so employment will not increase. The only impact of stimulative demand policies becomes rising prices. Another reason expansionary economic policy will fail to lower unemployment, as Barro (1974) points out, concerns the effects of these policies on government debt. For Keynes, a tax cut will increase demand for goods and services, and thereby increase hiring. But, as we saw above, tax cuts also lead to larger government deficits. According to rational expectations macroeconomics, citizens will realize that these deficits must be paid back in the future and that this will require higher taxes. People will therefore save most of their tax cut so that they can pay their higher taxes in the future. Tax cuts no longer increase consumer spending and employment; instead, saving is stimulated and deficits crowd out consumption.

A Post Keynesian theory of the state

Post Keynesians have responded to these two critiques of Keynes. In doing so, they have built upon the insights of Keynes and developed a Post Keynesian theory of the state. This theory provides a justification for activist fiscal policies.

One major problem with both critiques of Keynesian policy is that they rely on the traditional assumptions made in economic theory. These were the same assumptions that led economists to believe in a full employment equilibrium and that Keynes spent so much time and effort trying to counter. Keynes was particularly concerned with the assumptions that individual economic actors are thought to be rational and to have near-perfect knowledge about how the economy works. Neither of these assumptions accurately describes the real world.

Sen (1976/77), along with others, has pointed out the irrationality of the rationality assumption. To take just one example, individuals should expect to receive no gain from voting in political elections. The chances that my vote will decide the outcome of any election are minuscule. In fact, the likelihood of my getting struck by lightning while waiting in line to vote is greater than the probability that my vote will decide an election. However, if people do not vote, they do not get the democratic form of government and the voice in government that they desire. The Prisoner's Dilemma and other game theoretical paradoxes also cast doubt on the self-consistency of assuming rational, self-interested behavior (see Selten, 1978). These paradoxes demonstrate that individual rationality does not lead to the most optimal outcome for all individuals, or to group rationality.

Empirical psychology provides additional evidence against the rationality assumption as a description of how people actually behave. One established result is that judgments about potential risk are frequently mistaken and human fallibility tends to be greatest when people are most confident about their (faulty) judgment (Slovic *et al.*, 1982). For example, a large majority of people think that they will live past eighty (Weinstein, 1980) and that they, personally, are unlikely to be harmed by products they buy and use (Rethans, 1979).

Particularly damning for the rationality assumption is the phenomenon of preference reversal (see Slovic and Lichtenstein, 1983), where individual choice changes based upon *how* a set of alternatives gets presented (for example, describing the probability of "failure" rather than "success"). Psychologists refer to this as the "framing effect" (Tversky and Kahneman, 1986).

Neoclassical economists usually argue that these findings arise because artificial psychological experiments lack the learning incentives present in market activities. However, further work has found that greater incentives actually lead to *less* rational behavior (Tversky and Kahneman, 1986). Moreover, evidence from financial markets, where enormous sums of money can get made or lost and the incentives to rationality are greatest, supports the psychological literature.

There is a great deal of evidence against the rationality of players in financial markets. Shiller (2000) shows that security prices fluctuate based on fashion or mob psychology rather than the rational use of all available information. And Pressman (1998) has argued that the prevalence of financial frauds casts doubt on the rationality of investors in financial markets. If the rationality assumption fails to hold in financial markets, where conditions are most favorable, we should not expect it to hold in the political arena, which is not market-like and where the incentives to economic rationality are much weaker.

Furthermore, even if we accept the rationality assumption, this does not mean that state policy-makers will not seek to improve macroeconomic well-being. Self-interested individuals care about more than just money. Prestige, how history will view them, etc. are also motivating factors. If social approval is important for policy-makers, then self-interest will lead them to act for the public good since they are seeking public approval. And people who receive great utility from social approval and the verdict of history are more likely to become politicians.

One can also question Buchanan's assumptions about who goes into government and wants to be a policy-maker. He contends that those with a social agenda will seek government policy jobs and that their social agenda will be to increase government spending. But there are also people whose social agenda is to reduce government spending and reduce the role of government. Isn't this what the Reagan and Thatcher revolutions were all about? Moreover, those people who desire most to reduce the role of government will likely have the most money. And those without their own money will need financial support from others to accede to high public office with policy-making authority. Contra Buchanan, if we examine the predisposition of government officials, they are as likely to lean towards *less* government as much towards more government.

In addition to the failure of the rationality assumption, the existence of fundamental uncertainty (see Chapter 6) undermines the arguments of the rational expectations school and the public choice approach. If the economic environment is characterized by uncertainty then, in contrast to the claims of Buchanan, policy-makers will have difficulty discerning what is in their self-interest. Rather, as pointed out by Keynes ([1936] 1964: 383), they are likely to follow the dictates of some defunct economist who is currently in fashion. As a result, what is fashionable among economists and politicians becomes important. Similarly, if individual economic actors face an uncertain future, rational expectations cannot render fiscal policy ineffective. Contrary to the claims of Lucas, unemployed workers are not likely to know the inflationary impact of any policy change. And under these conditions, fiscal policy may be more effective if it creates expectations of better economic performance in the future and thereby leads to greater spending in the private sector.

Keynes ([1921] 1962) originally held that people were generally rational, but later came to reject this view when he saw that "people simply lacked the logical ability or rationality to see what was there" (Bateman, 1996: 56). When there is no scientific basic for making rational judgments or forming expectations about the future, because the future is uncertain, Keynes thought we must fall back on habits, instincts, and social convention, which are not rational in the economic sense of the term (Keynes, 1979: 294, also see Davis, 1994). In an uncertain and complex world, no one has extensive experience in making important decisions. To be able to navigate in such a world, people look around and see what others are doing. Behavior is imitative; we follow the behavior of others, which depends on the behavior of yet other people.

Faced with uncertainty, Post Keynesians see human behavior as driven by habits, institutions, herd behavior, and "animal spirits". In some instances we cannot make any predictions about the consequences of our actions because the future is so uncertain. In other situations we follow the herd, knowing that there is comfort in numbers. Consequently, for Post Keynesians preferences are not given as traditional economic theory holds. Rather, preferences are formed during the decision-making process because in an uncertain world the consequences of most actions are unknowable, so economic agents form expectations via social convention. These expectations then drive behavior and spending propensities. As a result, they also affect economic performance, according to Keynes ([1936] 1964, 1937, 1979), and can keep economies from achieving full employment.

Post Keynesians have adopted a behavioral theory of decision-making in their economic analysis. Rather than following the dictates of the rationality assumption, they see people as following rules of thumb. Workers spend large fractions of their labor income (if not all of it) based on habit and custom (as well as the fact that their pay, habitually, is only enough to cover their basic needs). Firms also follow rules of thumb in pricing (fixed markups or target pricing) rather than setting price equal to marginal cost (see Chapter 3).

Keynes saw the state as a set of institutions working for the public good. It provides public goods and benefits. In particular, the state must make sure that the requisite amount of spending takes place, leading to full employment and robust economic growth. The state must also control the national currency and back it. These are the key policy recommendations of the *General Theory*.

There are several reasons that the institution of the state is needed. Skidelsky (1989) argues that state policy is justified based on co-ordination failures at the macroeconomic level. If desired savings exceeded desired investment, the economy would contract without state economic policy to increase demand. Second, institutions help convert uncertainty into calculable risk for individuals (Giddens, 1991). The state provides laws and sets of regulations. These provide the necessary order for capitalist production to take place. In addition, the state provides for stability and security in life. This includes monetary stability, exchange rate stability, anti-trust legislation, welfare benefits, old-age benefits, etc. The welfare state is based on the idea that it is not enough to rely just on the market plus family and social networks.

One important rule concerns the national budget. When unemployment rises, national budgets get squeezed from two sides. First, there are the automatic stabilizers or spending programs that kick in. Unemployment insurance rises, social welfare spending increases, and workers tend to retire if possible. All of this increases spending by the state. On the other hand, when unemployment rises, the state collects less revenue through taxes. Both the increase in state spending and the reduction in state revenues cause the state budget to run in the red. One usual response to this is for the state to cut back on its expenditures and raise taxes. What Keynes pointed out was that such actions by the state would only make problems worse. What was needed, instead, was for the state to incur *even greater* deficits when unemployment was high and rising. It needed to stimulate demand through tax cuts and spending increases.

These views of Keynes and the Post Keynesians on the role of the state do receive empirical support. History provides a sort of controlled experiment that enables us to test the effectiveness of government policy-making. Before the advent of Keynesian economics governments did not attempt to manage the macroeconomy. Nor did they employ budget deficits as a tool to lower unemployment and stimulate economic growth. After Keynes, it has been regarded as the responsibility of governments to assure that the macroeconomy performs in a satisfactory fashion. Governments that fail inevitably get thrown out of office; governments that succeed generally continue in office.

Christine Roemer (1999) recently compared US business cycles prior to World War I and after World War II. She found that recessions were less frequent (because expansions were greater) in the latter time period and that the business cycle was 15 to 20 percent less volatile in the 50 years following World War II. Moreover, the output loss in the pre-World War I period was 6 percent greater than in the post-World War II period. Roemer (1999: 33) concludes these changes are likely due to "the rise of macroeconomic policy after World War II"– the use of monetary policy, discretionary fiscal policy, automatic or built-in stabilizers, and institutional changes like deposit insurance.

In a couple of papers, Pressman (1994, 1995) examined the macroeconomic performance of several developed economies since World War II based upon whether or not they tended to follow the policy advice of Keynes. He found that economic performance has been better whenever governments have run deficits in a manner similar to what Keynes recommended. In contrast, the stagflation of the 1970s and the slow growth of the 1980s was due to a failure to employ Keynesian fiscal policies. During these decades, governments focused more on reducing their budget deficits than on expanding them when economic growth slowed. The 1990s further support this view. As European nations lowered their budget deficits in anticipation of moving to a single currency (the Euro), their unemployment rates remained high. In contrast, the US was under no such pressure and economic growth expanded, leading to large budget surpluses.

Finally, there is the empirical issue of whether budget deficits crowd out business investment or other private spending. Examining whether large budget deficits lead to higher interest rates and less business investment, Eisner (1986) found that deficits tend to increase (or "crowd-in") business investment rather than reduce investment. He attributes this to the positive impact of deficits to the greater willingness of firms to invest in times of economic growth. Similarly,

Pressman (1995) found that government investment spending of the sort advocated by Keynes did not lead to either higher interest rates or lower private spending of any kind.

In sum, the available evidence tends to support the Post Keynesian position on the role of the state. In the real world policy actions have improved economic performance, and government budget deficits have not had negative economic effects. Rather, by not running larger structural deficits countries run the risk of continued economic stagnation. Consequently, even if policy-makers are entirely self-interested and rational, based on the evidence before them they should employ Keynesian or Post Keynesian economic policies. At some point, politicians and policy-makers must subject themselves and their views to the jury of public opinion. It is here that public perceptions of the effectiveness of public policy becomes important. Good public policy rewards politicians and their views on state policy.

Policy implications

The previous section argued that people are not as rational as neoclassical theory makes them out to be. They systematically make mistakes as they confront an uncertain world. Post Keynesians see the state as an uncertainty-reducing institution. By reducing uncertainty, the state is able to increase confidence and improve economic performance.

Correct budgetary policy is an important uncertainty-reducing institution. It gives business firms the confidence to invest and expand their operations, knowing that the production that ultimately results from this investment will be sold and will generate profits. A healthy economy in the future makes it more likely that firms will adopt an optimistic set of expectations and invest more. Budget policy contributes to this by assuring that demand is increased in bad economic times and reduced in good times.

A few policy proposals follow from the Post Keynesian analysis. First, the state must assume responsibility for overall economic performance. It must do this because without proper state action, economic problems will continue rather than correct themselves. Problems will persist because people are not as rational as the rational expectations view makes them out to be. State officials must also assume responsibility for overall economic performance because, contra Buchanan, it is in the interest of politicians to do so.

Second, there is the issue of budget policy. Correct state policy on the budget requires state surpluses in times of rapid growth, high employment and fears of inflation. In times of recession and high unemployment, the state needs to spend more and cut taxes, thereby raising a deficit that already exists due to poor economic circumstances.[1]

Note

1 The author thanks Ric Holt and Mark Setterfield for their comments on earlier versions of this paper. The usual caveats apply.

112   *Steven Pressman*

References

Barro, R. (1974) "Are Government Bonds Net Worth?" *Journal of Political Economy*, 82: 1095–117.

Bateman, B. (1996) *Keynes's Uncertain Revolution*, Ann Arbor: University of Michigan Press.

Buchanan, J. (1958) *Public Principles of Public Debt*, Homewood, IL: Richard D. Irwin.

Buchanan, J. and Wagner, R.E. (1977) *Democracy in Deficit: The Legacy of Lord Keynes*, New York: Academic Press.

Buchanan, J., Burton, J. and Wagner, R.E. (1978) *The Consequences of Mr. Keynes*, Institute of Economic Affairs.

Cornwall, J. (1994) *Economic Breakdown and Recovery*, Armonk, NY: M.E. Sharpe.

Davis, J. (1994) *Keynes's Philosophical Development*, Cambridge: Cambridge University Press.

Eichner, A.S. (ed.) (1978) *A Guide to Post Keynesian Economics*, Armonk, NY: M.E. Sharpe.

Eisner, R. (1986) *How Real Is the Federal Deficit?* New York: Free Press.

Friedman, M. (1962) *Capitalism and Freedom*, Chicago: University of Chicago Press.

Giddens, A. (1991) *Modernity and Self-Identity: Self and Society in the Late Modern Age*, Cambridge: Polity Press.

Hayek, F. (1944) *The Road to Serfdom*, Chicago: University of Chicago Press.

Keynes, J.M. [1921] (1962) *A Treatise on Probability*, New York: Harper & Row.

Keynes, J.M. [1936] (1964) *General Theory of Employment, Interest and Money*, New York: Harcourt, Brace & World.

Keynes, J.M. (1937) "The General Theory of Employment," *Quarterly Journal of Economics*, 51: 209–23.

Keynes, J.M. (1979) *The General Theory and After: Part II, Defense and Development*, The Collected Writings of John Maynard Keynes, vol. XXIX, London: Macmillan.

Lucas, R. (1976) "Econometric Policy Evaluation: A Critique," in K. Brunner and A. Meltzer (eds.) *The Phillips Curve and Labor Markets*, Amsterdam, North Holland, pp. 19–46.

Lucas, R. and Sargent, T. (1978) "After Keynesian Macroeconomics," in *After the Phillips Curve: Persistence of High Inflation and High Unemployment*, Boston: Federal Reserve Bank of Boston, pp. 49–72.

Pressman, S. (1994) "The Composition of Government Spending: Does It Make Any Difference?" *Review of Political Economy*, 6: 221–39.

Pressman, S. (1995) "Deficits, Full Employment and the Use of Fiscal Policy," *Review of Political Economy*, 7: 212–26.

Pressman, S. (1998) "On Financial Frauds and their Causes," *American Journal of Economics and Sociology*, 57: 405–21.

Rethans, A. (1979) *An Investigation of Consumer Perceptions of Product Hazards*. PhD dissertation, University of Oregon.

Roemer, C. (1999) "Changes in Business Cycles: Evidence and Explanations," *Journal of Economic Perspectives*, 23–44.

Selten, R. (1978) "The Chain Store Paradox," *Theory and Decision*, 9: 127–59.

Sen, A. (1976/77) "Rational Fools: A Critique of the Behavioral Foundations of Economic Theory," *Philosophy and Public Affairs*, 6: 317–44.

Shiller, R. (2000) *Irrational Exuberance*, Princeton: Princeton University Press.

Skidelsky, R. (1989) "Keynes and the State," in D. Helm (ed.) *The Economic Borders of the State*, Oxford: Oxford University Press, pp. 144–52.

Slovic, P. and Lichtenstein, S. (1983) "Preference Reversals: A Broader Perspective," *American Economic Review*, 72: 923–55.

Slovic, P., Fischhoff, B. and Lichtenstein, S. (1982) "Facts versus Fears: Understanding Perceived Risk" in D. Kahneman, P. Slovic and A. Tversky (eds) *Judgment under Uncertainty: Heruistics and Biases*, New York: Cambridge University Press, pp. 463–89.

Tversky, A. and Kahneman, D. (1986) "Rational Choice and the Framing of Decisions," in R.M. Hogarth and M.W. Reder (eds.) *Rational Choice: The Contrast between Economics and Psychology*, Chicago: University of Chicago Press, pp. 67–94.

Weinstein, N.D. "Unrealistic Optimism About Future Life Events," *Journal of Personality and Social Psychology*, 39: 806–20.

11 International monetary arrangements

John Smithin

Introduction

In the first *Guide to Post Keynesian Economics,* Burbridge (1978) wrote the chapter on international economic issues. He concentrated primarily on trade theory and conceded that Post Keynesians had not yet constructed a formal trade model to rival the venerable neoclassical edifice.

This relative neglect of international monetary affairs might be attributed to the fact that Post Keynesian theory was originally formulated to describe closed economies. Another factor, perhaps, was the historical circumstances at the time of publication. Bretton Woods collapsed in the early 1970s, but our modern concerns with global capital markets and international financial instability had not yet come to the fore.

As time has moved on, and as international economic issues have become more important, economists have had to pay more attention to the rise of the global economy. And Post Keynesians have been deeply concerned with issues of globalization (see Dow, 1999 for a survey). However, to date, no consensus has emerged, comparable to the Post Keynesian consensus regarding the closed economy.

The reasons for a certain lack of consensus are not difficult to discern. On the one hand, Post Keynesians stress the problem of fundamental uncertainty (as opposed to probabilistic risk), in capitalist economies (see Chapter 6). In the international context, wildly fluctuating exchange rates, large and unpredictable speculative movements of financial capital, payments imbalances, and unequal debt burdens all increase uncertainty and instability. Post Keynesian analysts would therefore tend to favor measures that reduce uncertainty and make the international environment less turbulent. These measures might include capital controls, fixed exchange rates, and the establishment of powerful supra-national regulatory and central banking institutions to supervise the international system.

On the other hand, Post Keynesians also insist on macroeconomic management to ensure full employment and general prosperity. The problem is that some measures designed to promote stability on the international level (such as fixed exchange rates) may restrict the ability of individual governments to pursue macroeconomic policy at the national level. This tension would be resolved if a world government or world monetary authority could be relied upon to pursue global policies that ensured full employment and general prosperity. But this is a very large if; it also raises political, social, and cultural concerns about a "new world order."

The next section contains a brief history of the international monetary system. Then we discuss the two main Post Keynesian responses to globalization. The first seeks an international solution to international problems, including international financial institutions and greater regulation of exchange rate parities and capital flows. The model here would be Keynes's International Clearing Union (ICU) proposal of the 1940s, or the Bretton Woods system of 1944–71. The second type of response takes a more nationalistic line. It insists on measures that allow national jurisdictions to pursue Keynesian expansionary policies within their own borders. Keynes (1982: 236) supported this policy stance in the 1930s when he advocated that "finance be primarily national."[1]

Development of the international monetary system

Problems of international finance arise in a world with more than one monetary asset and where international trade takes place. This raises issues of exchange rate determination, interest rate policy in each center, and how economic growth is financed. Historically, different monetary assets have been identified with different national political boundaries, but contemporary experience demonstrates that a particular monetary standard need not be restricted to domestic residents.

In practice, the world economy has often been dominated by the central bank of one particularly strong nation. This institution becomes effectively the world central bank, and its liabilities the international reserve currency. Its decisions determine the availability of financial resources to the system as a whole. Obvious examples would be the nineteenth-century Bank of England, the US Federal Reserve in the mid-twentieth century, and (in a regional context) the German Bundesbank in Europe during the 1980s and 1990s. The rise to financial power seems to follow from a country building up a net credit position with its trading partners. However, a considerable element of inertia also exists in the process. Although economic strength is a prerequisite for a national currency to acquire reserve currency status, at times national currencies have continued to play an international role after the power of the host country has begun to wane, thus damaging the stability of the system.

There has always been debate about whether exchange rates should be floating or fixed. Floating rates are determined by demand and supply on international financial markets. Under fixed rates, domestic and foreign central banks use direct intervention and interest rate changes to keep relative currency values within narrow bands. The managed or "dirty" float is a hybrid regime. Exchange rates float, but domestic authorities periodically intervene. A final possibility, as in contemporary Europe, pushes the concept of fixed exchange rates to its logical extreme in the form of a currency union.

As long as assets denominated in different currencies are not regarded as perfect substitutes, and exchange rates are free to move, there is room to maneuver on domestic interest rates; any discrepancies among national interest rates can be accommodated by exchange rate changes. A currency union eliminates national independence to control interest rates. Power over interest rates devolves to the supra-national central bank. The less extreme choice of a fixed exchange rate regime also means that individual economies must relinquish power over domestic interest rates. Unlike a currency union, however, a fixed exchange rate regime is not irrevocable. It is possible to negotiate periodic changes in par values. If all else fails, the domestic economy can quit the system and allow the exchange rate to float.

The international gold standard before 1914 was a classic example of a fixed rate regime. Each major currency was convertible into a fixed quantity of gold, implying *de facto* fixed exchange rates. This period is viewed with nostalgia by conservative advocates of "sound money," although the actual results in terms of economic stability remain subject to debate (Hicks, 1989).

In practice, there was never enough gold in existence for each country to pay out gold on demand. The system thus depended on a readily available gold substitute. This part was played by sterling, confidence in which depended on Britain being a major economic power and a creditor nation. When Britain became a debtor nation after World War I it was impossible to reconstruct the old system. The interwar period was one of global monetary disorder. Attempts to return to the gold standard collapsed disastrously in the international financial crisis of 1931, and the 1930s were a period of "beggar-thy-neighbor" competitive depreciation policies.

The Bretton Woods agreement of 1944 attempted to reintroduce stability to the system. However, the Bretton Woods era was by no means a new gold standard. Only the US dollar could be exchanged for gold, and only by central banks. Also, Bretton Woods was never as rigid as the gold standard. Exchange rates were fixed but adjustable, and there were extensive capital controls. The system survived until August 1971, when the US cut the link between gold and the dollar. By early 1973 the main currencies were floating, and the contemporary non-system was in place. The dollar retained a key role; but by the 1990s, the US dollar, the Japanese yen, and the German mark (now replaced by the Euro) were each important in different areas of the world.

Most commentators regard the performance of the international monetary system in the twentieth century as unsatisfactory. Volatile exchange rates combined with the globalization of financial markets, financial deregulation and liberalization, and technical change have greatly increased international capital movements. In balance of payments adjustment, the capital account, including speculative capital movements, tends to dominate the current account via exchange rate changes. Current account balances may no longer be perceived as deriving from genuine economic effort (e.g., surpluses arising when an economy becomes more competitive), but simply result as a byproduct of capital market activity.

During the 1990s, the exchange rate mechanism (ERM) crisis in 1992/93, the Mexican peso crisis of 1994–95, and the Asian currency crises of 1997–98, all increased concerns about the international monetary system. Although most of these episodes involved attempts to keep exchange rates "pegged" at inappropriate levels, it is nonetheless easy to understand renewed contemporary interest in restructuring the international monetary system.

The search for stability

Many Post Keynesians have typically supported fixed exchange rates. This is consistent with their other arguments favoring stability of nominal or money variables (Rogers, 1989). The argument is based on a familiar chain of reasoning. As stressed by Keynes (1936, 1937) and his Post Keynesian followers (e.g., Davidson, 1991a, 1994), decision-making in both national and international markets is hampered by pervasive uncertainty. In such an environment, inelastic expectations about the values of nominal variables can be an important stabilizing factor. Stable nominal exchange rates therefore recommend themselves in much the same way as do stable interest rates and stable nominal wages.

In a detailed analysis, Pressman (1993: 95–101) provides at least five reasons why flexible exchanges rate might be detrimental. First, volatile exchange rates can increase the cost of foreign trade and hence discourage trade. Second, the activities and energies of firms and entrepreneurs can be diverted towards speculation and finance instead of production. Third, the increase in uncertainty will discourage investment and hence productivity growth. Fourth, the domestic economy may be destabilized, as the contribution of net exports will itself be unstable. Fifth, volatile exchange rates may adversely affect labor's share of income, because capital is more internationally mobile than labor. Pressman also provides some empirical evidence that these adverse effects did show up in the G7 countries in the early 1970s after the breakdown of Bretton Woods and the move to floating exchanges rates. Economic performance along most dimensions did worsen in the 1970s and 1980s. However, as Pressman also points out, it is difficult to sort out empirically whether worsening economic performance was caused by the change to floating rates or simply coincided with it.

If Post Keynesians have tended to favor exchange rate stability during the second half of the twentieth century, many neoclassical economists favored flexible rates, regarding it the free-market solution. Following Friedman (1953), the standard arguments were that flexible rates would allow each country to determine its own national inflation rate (with lower inflation rates being regarded as the most desirable from this perspective), and that speculation would tend to be stabilizing rather than destabilizing.

However, the predilection of some twentieth century neoclassical economists for flexible exchange rates should not be exaggerated. This was definitely not the orthodox view during the nineteenth century and well into the first half of the twentieth century. "Sound money" in those days meant the international gold standard. More recently there has also been a return to these earlier attitudes. Some contemporary orthodox economists see fixed exchange rates as constraining national central banks (preventing them from inflating more than the average of the system as a whole) just as the old gold standard was supposed to do. In addition, most mainstream economists support the single currency project in Europe precisely because the European Central Bank (ECB) is mandated to prevent inflation. So it would hardly be correct to identify support for greater exchange rate stability with Post Keynesian economics and support for flexible rates with neoclassical economics (or vice versa). To a large extent this particular debate cuts across party lines (Smithin, 1991).

One issue on which there is clear disagreement between Post Keynesian economists and their neoclassical counterparts is the desirability of greater capital flows. Recently, greater capital flows have resulted from deregulation, technical change, and the globalization of financial markets. Neoclassical economists tend to see this as a good thing, enhancing the power of market forces. Post Keynesian economists generally take the opposite view (Eatwell, 1996; Palley, 1998; Michie and Grieve-Smith, 1999). They see increased capital mobility as destabilizing rather than stabilizing. It increases the likelihood of crisis, makes domestic macroeconomic management more difficult, and penalizes poorer countries. Hence, there have been a number of suggestions that capital controls could usefully be reintroduced, either at the national or the international level. Among the devices that could be used are quantitative restrictions on the export of capital (such as a system of capital export licenses), minimum stay requirements on the import of capital,[2] and more effective regulation of short sales of a national currency (Palley, 1998).

One moderate proposal that has received a great deal of attention is the Tobin Tax. James Tobin (1978) proposed a levy of 1.25% on *all* international capital transactions. This would penalize speculative short-term capital movements, and hence contribute to stability, but at the same time not discourage long-term capital investments. The tax might also raise substantial revenue and perhaps finance international development projects (Palley, 1998; Arestis and Sawyer, 1999).

Other practical suggestions put forward by Post Keynesians for stabilizing the contemporary international financial environment draw inspiration from those actually on the table in the negotiations leading up to the Bretton Woods system. It is indisputable that the Bretton Woods era coincided with a period of satisfactory macroeconomic performance in most jurisdictions. So it is not unreasonable to think that the institutional structure established at Bretton Woods in some way contributed to this favorable economic climate (Pressman, 1993; Eatwell, 1996). In the current search for greater international financial stability, an obvious starting point is to adapt something along the lines of Keynes's ICU, or a new Bretton Woods. This would typically involve an international agency of some kind, possibly issuing an international currency for use in balance of payments settlement, fixed but adjustable exchange rates between the major players, and a clear set of rules (which may include capital controls) designed to ensure the smooth operation of the system.

A number of variants on this outline are possible, and various choices need to be made in designing the system. Davidson (1991b, 1994, 1996) sets forth a detailed set of proposals in the tradition of Keynes's plan for an ICU. He advocates creating an international "unionized" monetary system (UMS) in which national currencies are locked together via fixed exchange rates. There would also be an international clearing agency to clear net balances between countries in terms of an international money clearing unit (IMCU), which would be money for these purposes only. Exchange rates would be fixed in terms of the ICMU, but (as under Bretton Woods) they would be adjustable if unit costs in different countries got too far out of line.

Grieve-Smith (1997, 1999) has put forward a ten-point plan along the lines of Bretton Woods, in essence a new managed exchange rate regime. One distinctive feature of this proposal is that changes in parities be "relatively small and frequent" (1997: 221–2) rather than traumatic political crises as they often have been in the past. Grieve-Smith (1999) also advocates establishing a new international stabilization fund with large resources and a mandate to intervene automatically in support of agreed upon parities. The plan would also include strong measures (involving taxation) to curb speculative capital movements, and the international regulation and supervision of financial institutions.

When Post Keynesians advocate creating new institutional structures, and potentially powerful international agencies to serve as a global central bank or regulator of capital flows and exchanges (Dow, 1999), they naturally assume that policy-makers will have global full employment as their primary objective and that they will actively pursue expansionary policies. However, Smithin and Wolf (1993, 1999) have pointed out that international bureaucracies may not play the part written for them. Historical examples are not encouraging in this respect. Keynes, after all, was one of the principal architects of the IMF, an institution that has not been particularly imbued with the Keynesian spirit. Another potential problem is democratic accountability. Any new agency powerful enough to perform the job demanded of it must play a dominating role in global monetary policy, with a corresponding weakening of power at the national level.

Keynesianism in one country?

Although relatively fixed exchange rates are often associated with the Post Keynesian position, there is another traditional line of thought on this question. This is, that if national governments, as opposed to an international agency, are to pursue Keynesian policies, they cannot commit themselves in advance to fixed parities. With fixed rates, the balance of payments, rather than domestic output and employment, becomes the primary object of attention for domestic policy-makers. Expansionary policy in a single country can be brought to a premature end by balance of payments difficulties. There have been several real world instances of this, including the famous "U turn" by the Mitterand government in France in 1983 (Parguez, 1993). Therefore, writing in the British context shortly after the break-up of Bretton Woods, Skidelsky (1975: 106) expressed a widespread view when he wrote, "we may be more inclined to date the triumph of the Keynesian revolution from 1972 when Britain floated the pound, rather than from 1945; and to see this too not as a culmination but as a new beginning." Similar views have been expressed at different times by such writers as Lerner (1983), Kaldor (1986), and, more recently, Smithin (1999).

The ability to pursue independent macroeconomic policy obviously does not ensure that Keynesian policies will be implemented. Rather the point is that national authorities would at least be *free* to implement such policies, and that popular political pressure might more easily be brought to bear in the national, rather than the international, context. For advocates of independent national policy-making, the best-case scenario would be coordinated expansionary policies in a number of jurisdictions simultaneously. This would foster world growth, and still allow for reasonable exchange rate stability and approximate balance of the capital and current accounts across jurisdictions. The worst-case scenario would be one where most countries were not taking such action, and perhaps pursuing deflation. But even in this case it would be possible for one or two nations to escape global pressures by taking a contrarian stance. Contrarian nations would have faster growth, lower unemployment, a real depreciation of the currency, and current account surpluses, albeit at the expense of their partners who would be in deficit (Paschakis and Smithin, 1998; Smithin, 2001). In any event, "Keynesianism in one country," to borrow a phrase used by Tarshis (1989),[3] does seem to require some freedom of action in terms of exchange rate policy.

Unlike the situation facing Keynes in the 1920s or Kaldor in the 1960s, the environment today is greatly complicated by the globalization of capital markets. A claim heard frequently in both the popular and financial press is that monetary authorities can no longer influence economic events in their own country. The argument is that the modern world is at the mercy of capricious global economic forces, including massive speculative movements of capital, leaving little choice but to follow the dictates of international market forces. In such a world, the idea of separate monetary systems and national macroeconomic policy seems to become obsolete. This could be interpreted, somewhat ironically, as an argument for both fixed exchange rates and new international regulatory agencies on the grounds that there is really no other viable structure for economic governance.

The debate over capital controls is once again relevant to the problem; one way of "putting the genie back in the bottle" is to re-establish controls on the capital movements perceived to cause the problem. For example, Palley (1998: 184–93) argues that we should retain a flexible exchange rate system, but limit capital mobility via capital controls of some kind. This would maximize the ability of individual nations to pursue an independent policy. This is the "right way to go" for Post Keynesians according to the author. In contrast, the current system has exchange rate flexibility, but domestic policy options are limited by footloose capital. Fixed exchange rates combined with capital mobility, which may well be the preferred option of many conservative economists, would be a twenty-first century version of the old gold standard, complete with the traditional deflationary bias. The final possibility, a new Bretton Woods type arrangement with capital controls and fixed exchange rates also has its disadvantages from this point of view. Capital controls enhance the possibility of policies suited to local conditions, but the fixed exchange rate element militates against them. Bretton Woods was successful for a time, but this may have been a result of the expansionary instincts of the main player, the US (Smithin, 1996), rather than its formal structure. Eventually the fixed parities could not be sustained and the system broke up.

The situation discussed by Palley is often referred to as the "inconsistent trio" of capital mobility, fixed exchange rates, and national autonomy in the conduct of monetary policy. The argument is that it is possible to have any two of these, but not all three. Conservatives usually argue that option three must be abandoned in the modern world (Padoa-Schioppa, 1988).[4] In a very real sense, the single European currency represents the apotheosis of this kind of thinking. But Palley argues that there is no particular merit in either of the first two.

Taking a slightly different tack, Smithin and Wolf (1993, 1999) argue that even if it is impossible to reintroduce capital controls, domestic authorities might still be able to pursue Keynesian policies as long as they have the necessary political will. The authors accept that the globalization of financial markets and increasing international capital flows move the world closer to the textbook case of perfect capital mobility. Nonetheless, they point out that as long as there are separate national monetary systems and exchange rates are potentially free to move, the purely technical changes in themselves are not likely to induce speculators to treat different financial assets as perfect substitutes. However, it is perfect asset substitutability (rather than simply perfect capital mobility) that is required for domestic authorities to legitimately claim that they have "no choice" but to submit to the dictates of the international capital markets.

Paraskevopoulos *et al.* (1996) and Paschakis and Smithin (1998) show that a mechanism does exist whereby a small or medium-sized open economy can achieve monetary sovereignty even with free capital mobility. The argument rests on the distinction between capital flight and capital outflow, and the potentially beneficial impact of an increase in a nation's foreign credit position on the risk premium demanded by foreign investors. Although an expansionary policy may lead to capital outflow, this not necessarily a bad thing for the "credit rating" of the country. If capital outflow does not become capital flight, the outflow builds up a net credit position with the rest of the world. To the extent that the promises to pay of creditor nations are more trustworthy than those of debtors, this may improve the international status of the currency rather damage it. If so, a paradoxical Keynesian virtuous cycle may arise in nations prepared to pursue expansionary policies and give priority to domestic output and employment outcomes, rather than to take a deflationary stance perceived as more palatable to international financiers.

At least for those countries with sufficient credit to issue debt denominated in domestic currency, and which maintain low but positive real rates of interest, the suggested mechanism repairs a gap in the Keynesian case for cheap money and expansionary policy in a single country. Judicious policy can manipulate the risk premium on assets denominated in the domestic currency. The existence of a risk premium to be manipulated, however, does imply the continued existence of separate monetary systems and exchange rates that are free to change, even if they are stable in practice and not actually expected to change. In terms of the inconsistent trio, if capital mobility is a fact of life under globalization but national autonomy remains desirable, national authorities must retain some freedom of action over exchange rates and resist commitments to fix parities or to join a currency union.

Concluding remarks

Following the above discussion, one might ask whether there is any unified Post Keynesian approach to international finance. As we have seen, there is no agreement on any *particular* proposal for reform of the international financial architecture. For example, some Post Keynesians support initiatives such as the Tobin Tax, whereas others have written against them. Nor is there agreement on the merits of a given exchange rate policy in all circumstances. There has been a tendency for Post Keynesian economists to favor stable exchange rates, but most have opposed monetary union in Europe, which might seem the logical endpoint of such a stance.

Nonetheless, it can be argued that there are at least five broad principles on which most Post Keynesian economists would probably agree concerning international finance.

First, exchange rate regimes and international financial institutions are not ends in themselves but are means to an end. The ultimate ends include global prosperity, full employment, and a more equitable distribution of income between individuals and between richer and poorer nations. International monetary arrangements should be evaluated based on whether or not they help achieve these goals.

Second, there would be little support for a *laissez-faire* solution simply because it is a free-market solution. The obvious example here is the willingness of many Post Keynesian economists to advocate capital controls. These would clearly interfere with market forces; yet many Post Keynesians believe that "throwing some sand in the gears" of international finance would improve the performance of global capitalism.

Third, Post Keynesians reject the air of inevitability which often characterizes discussions by both mainstream economists and the popular financial press on these issues. In particular, they reject the view that the process of globalization is in some sense inexorable or irreversible, like a force of nature, and that only certain types of economic organization or particular policy options are available in the modern world. Post Keynesians tend to believe that all issues, including international financial relations, are amenable to rational thought and management, and to the application of policy solutions arrived at by cooperation and consensus.

Fourth, Post Keynesians favor solutions that increase stability and decrease uncertainty in the international financial environment. Those advocating relatively fixed exchange rates do so on this basis. But Post Keynesians who argue against pre-commitment to any fixed set of exchange rate parities hardly favor volatility and instability. They favor managing exchange rates to secure policy objectives and to provide a more predictable environment for both foreign and domestic investors.

Finally, from the Post Keynesian perspective, international financial arrangements should enable policy-makers to conduct public policy. Arrangements should not be designed to impose constraints on the pursuit of full employment or other desirable goals. The gold standard was just such a constraining regime, whose supporters favored it precisely because they thought it would prevent any tendency towards inflationary policy on the part of any single player. Post Keynesian skepticism about the European single currency follows along these lines. Keynes's ICU proposal, on the other hand, was designed to facilitate economic expansion at the international level.

As to the policy implications of the Post Keynesian approach, there is likely to be more consensus on specific policy proposals than would appear at first sight. The issue is not ultimately a question of fixed versus flexible exchange rates, but whether a particular proposal conforms to the basic principles set out above. During the 1920s almost all Post Keynesians would have supported Keynes in opposing a return to the gold standard. During the Bretton Woods negotiations most would have supported the Keynes Plan over the White Plan.[5] More recently, most Post Keynesians have opposed European monetary union even though it eliminates exchange rate problems. Similarly, most Post Keynesians would have agreed, even before the Asian currency crises of 1997–98, that attempts to unilaterally "peg" exchange rates but allow free capital mobility are bound to lead to trouble.

It is probably also reasonable to assert that few Post Keynesians would object to any contemporary proposals that would genuinely restore stability to the exchanges, regulate capital flows, reduce payments imbalances, and improve global economic performance and income distribution. The caveats would be primarily on the grounds of the realities of global power politics, and such questions as nationalism versus internationalism, rather than economic principle.[6]

Notes

1 In the 1920s and 1930s, Keynes (1980: 16) seemed sympathetic to monetary sovereignty for national policy-makers. He even defended the final Bretton Woods settlement before the House of Lords in 1944 on the grounds that the international monetary arrangements

would enable the UK "to retain control of our own domestic rate of interest, so that we can keep it as low as suits our own purposes." Also see Smithin and Wolf (1993: 368–71).

2   Similar to those actually imposed in Chile during the 1990s.

3   This is an ironic reference to Stalin's "socialism in one country."

4   The author actually refers to the "inconsistent quartet" of free trade, full capital mobility, fixed exchange rates, and national autonomy in the conduct of monetary policy (Padoa-Schioppa, 1988: 373). Assuming a relatively liberal trading regime, this leaves the inconsistent trio mentioned in the text. Of course, the merits of free trade may also be disputed and debated.

5   The latter, named after Harry Dexter White, was the set of proposals on which the settlement was ultimately based.

6   I would like to thank the editors for the invitation to contribute to this volume, and for a number of well-directed criticisms of an earlier draft of this paper.

References

Arestis, P. and Sawyer, M. (1999) "What Role for the Tobin tax in World Economic Governance?" in J. Michie and J. Grieve-Smith (eds.) *Global Instability: the Political Economy of World Economic Governance*, London: Routledge, pp. 151–67.

Burbidge, J. (1978) "The International Dimension," in A.S. Eichner (ed.) *A Guide to Post Keynesian Economics*, Armonk, NY: M.E. Sharpe, pp. 139–50.

Davidson, P. (1991a) *Controversies in Post Keynesian Economics*, Aldershot: Edward Elgar.

Davidson, P. (1991b) "What International Payments Scheme Would Keynes Have Suggested for the Twenty-first Century?" in P. Davidson and J. Kregel (eds.) *Economic Problems of the 1990s: Europe, the Developing Countries, and the United States*, Aldershot: Edward Elgar, pp. 85–104.

Davidson, P. (1994) *Post Keynesian Macroeconomic Theory: A Foundation for Successful Economic Policies for the Twenty-First Century*, Aldershot: Edward Elgar.

Davidson, P. (1996) "Reforming the International Payments System," in R.A. Blecker (ed.), *US Trade Policy and Global Growth: New Directions in the International Economy*, Armonk, New York: M.E. Sharpe, pp. 215–36.

Dow, S.C. (1999) "International Liquidity Preference and Endogenous Credit Creation," in J.T. Harvey and J. Deprez (eds.), *Foundations of International Economics: Post Keynesian Perspectives*, London: Routledge, pp. 153–70.

Eatwell, J. (1996) "International Capital Liberalization: the Record," CEPA Working Paper no. 1, New School for Social Research.

Friedman, M. (1953) "The Case for Flexible Exchange Rates," in *Essays in Positive Economics*, Chicago: University of Chicago Press, pp. 157–203.

Grieve-Smith, J. (1997) *Full Employment: A Pledge Betrayed*, London: Macmillan.

Grieve-Smith, J. (1999) "A New Bretton Woods?" in J. Michie and J. Grieve-Smith (eds.) *Global Instability: the Political Economy of World Economic Governance*, London: Routledge, pp. 227–50.

Hicks, J. (1989) *A Market Theory of Money*, Oxford: Clarendon Press.

Kaldor, N. (1986) *The Scourge of Monetarism*, 2nd edition, Oxford: Oxford University Press.

Keynes, J.M. (1936) *The General Theory of Employment, Interest and Money*, London: Macmillan.

Keynes, J.M. (1937) "The General Theory of Employment," *Quarterly Journal of Economics*, 51: 209–33.

Keynes, J.M. (1980) *Activities 1941–46: Shaping the Post-War World: Reparations and Bretton Woods, The Collected Writings of John Maynard Keynes*, vol. XXVI, London: Macmillan.

Keynes, J.M. (1982) *Activities 1931–39: World Crises and Policies in Britain and America, The Collected Writings of John Maynard Keynes*, vol. XXI, London: Macmillan.

Lerner, A.P. (1983) *Selected Economic Writing of Abba P. Lerner*, D.C. Colander (ed.), New York: New York University Press.

Michie, J. and Grieve-Smith, J. (eds.) (1999) *Global Instability: The Political Economy of World Economic Governance*, London: Routledge.

Palley, T.I. (1998) *Plenty of Nothing: The Downsizing of the American Dream and the Case for Structural Keynesianism*, Princeton: Princeton University Press.

Padoa-Schioppa, T. (1988) "The European Monetary System: A Long-term View," in F. Giavazzi, S. Micossi and M. Miller (eds.) *The European Monetary System*, Cambridge: Cambridge University Press, pp. 369–84.

Paraskevopoulos, C.C., Paschakis, J. and Smithin, J. (1996) "Is Monetary Sovereignty an Option for the Small Open Economy?" *North American Journal of Economics and Finance*, 7: 5–18.

Parguez, A. (1993) "L'austérité Budgétaire en France," in P. Paquette and M. Seccareccia (eds.) *Les piéges de l'austérité*, Montreal, Les Presses de l'Université de Montréal, pp. 83–103.

Paschakis, J. and Smithin, J. (1998) "Exchange Risk and the Supply Side Effect of Real Exchange Rate Changes," *Journal of Macroeconomics*, 20: 703–20.

Pressman, S. (1993) "The Macroeconomic Effects of Exchange Rate Instability," in I.H. Rima (ed.) *The Political Economy of Global Restructuring*, vol. II, Aldershot: Edward Elgar, pp. 91–103.

Rogers, C. (1989) *Money, Interest and Capital: A Study in the Foundations of Monetary Theory*, Cambridge: Cambridge University Press.

Skidelsky, R. (1975) "The Reception of the Keynesian Revolution," in M. Keynes (ed.) *Essays on John Maynard Keynes*, Cambridge: Cambridge University Press, pp. 89–107.

Smithin, J. (1991) "European Monetary Arrangements and National Economic Sovereignty," in A. Amin and M. Dietrich (eds.) *Towards a New Europe? Structural Change in the European Economy*, Aldershot: Edward Elgar, pp. 191–211.

Smithin, J. (1996) *Macroeconomic Policy and the Future of Capitalism: The Revenge of the Rentiers and the Threat to Prosperity*, Aldershot: Edward Elgar.

Smithin, J. (1999) "Money and National Sovereignty in the Global Economy," *Eastern Economic Journal*, 25: 49–61.

Smithin, J. (2001) "Monetary Autonomy and Financial Integration," in L.P. Rochon and M. Vernengo (eds.) *Credit, Interest Rates and the Open Economy: Essays on Horizontalism*, Cheltenham: Edward Elgar, 243–55.

Smithin, J. and Wolf, B.M. (1993) "What Would be a 'Keynesian' Approach to Currency and Exchange Rate Issues?" *Review of Political Economy*, 5: 365–83.

Smithin, J. and Wolf, B.M. (1999) "A World Central Bank?" in J. Michie and J. Grieve-Smith (eds.) *Global Instability: The Political Economy of World Economic Governance*, London: Macmillan, pp. 212–26.

Tarshis, L. (1989) "Keynesianism in a Single Country: Can it Work?" mimeo, Glendon College.

Tobin, J. (1978) "A Proposal for International Monetary Reform," *Eastern Economic Journal*, 4: 153–59.

12 A look ahead

Richard P.F. Holt and Steven Pressman

When he edited the first Post Keynesian *Guide*, Alfred Eichner (1978) was convinced that economics needed a paradigm shift. He was very critical of neoclassical economics, believing that it lacked empirical content and perpetuated a myth that the market is a self-regulating mechanism. He also believed that Post Keynesian economics provided a serious alternative to neoclassical theory. However, he was not optimistic that mainstream economics would accept the Post Keynesian paradigm.

Eichner's prediction turned out to be true. After the collapse of the neoclassical synthesis in the 1970s a classical counter-revolution took hold, one which has dominated the economics profession ever since. In the 1990s New Keynesian macroeconomics attempted to develop an alternative to new classical theory. But little in New Keynesian economics is either new or Keynesian in nature; and New Keynesianism has not broken the hold of new classical economics on macroeconomic theory.

Post Keynesian economics has not been dormant or irrelevant while these battles have raged. Substantial progress has been made in developing the Post Keynesian paradigm over the past twenty or so years. Besides its primary objective of carrying out the theoretical implications of the Keynesian revolution, Post Keynesian economics has been able to expand its perspective by relying on the writings of Michal Kalecki and the institutionalists. It has also developed new areas of research. Because of this effort there is now a distinct Post Keynesian methodology plus a coherent and consistent theoretical approach. This volume explains the Post Keynesian paradigm in a manner that we hope is accessible to both students and interested economists.

As we noted in Chapter 1, the challenges now facing Post Keynesians are different from those when the first *Guide* was published. In addition to the rise of new classical macroeconomics, the past two decades have witnessed dramatic economic and social changes, such as the collapse of the former Soviet Union, the liberalization of financial markets, and globalization. With these changes has also come a different attitude about economic policy and the role of government. Beginning in the 1980s, government intervention in industrialized economies has been scaled back and replaced by policies of privatization and deregulation. Yet the problems facing an interdependent world economy, problems that require government policy interventions, are greater than ever.

Given these circumstances, it is now important for Post Keynesians to go beyond theory and focus more on public policy, empirical analysis, and looking at the effects of economic globalization. Perhaps the greatest challenge for Post Keynesians is to provide relevant economic policies for the problems of the twenty-first century. They also need to develop empirical evidence and arguments that support their views on how the economic world works. Finally, Post Keynesian economists must expand their horizons and analysis so that they are applicable to a global, interdependent world economy. Clearly, there is much work that remains to be done.

For starters, Post Keynesians need to put more effort into exploring traditional microeconomic policy issues. This shift is needed for two reasons. First, Post Keynesians have solved most of the macroeconomic problems that concerned them. Second, many important policy issues in the world economy today are microeconomic in nature and Post Keynesian economists proudly proclaim that they are interested in the real world. Let us consider a few of these problems.

Most of the developed world is facing an aging population in the twenty-first century. This will require that we have adequate resources in the future to support an elderly population that is not working or producing goods. The neoclassical view sees current savings as the answer to the problem of how we get more goods for tomorrow. Saving generates investment, which in turn, increases our productive capabilities. The paradox of thrift is forgotten or ignored on this traditional way of thinking. Post Keynesians see traditional analysis as putting the cart before the horse; they regard investment as the cause of savings (Gordon, 1995; Palley, 1996). But saying this does not help deal with the problem of an aging population. We still need a set of policy proposals that will enable us to support a much larger group of retired people at decent living standards in the not-too-distant future.

A second, related, concern is productivity. Productivity growth fell in all developed countries beginning in the 1970s and, except for the US during the late 1990s, has failed to return to anything approaching its high levels of the 1950s and 1960s. Standard economic theory tends to blame excessive government regulation as well as the lack of savings (and hence lack of investment) for the productivity slowdown. But this view receives little empirical support. Strikingly, the massive deregulation effort begun in the 1980s failed to revive productivity growth. And as noted in the previous paragraph, Post Keynesians realize that more savings cannot cause more investment because it is the consequence of greater investment rather than its cause. Again, it is one thing to point out flaws with the standard policy proposals of neoclassical economists; what is more important is to have an alternative analysis of the productivity slowdown based on Post Keynesian theory and also a set of policy proposals that, if instituted, might revive productivity growth.

To take a third example, most neoclassical theory extols the virtues of markets. Yet for one of the most important goods that we consume, education, there is pretty much a monopoly supplier (the government) not subject to the discipline of the market. The major neoclassical policy proposal follows quite simply from this analysis – education vouchers will force schools to compete for students and will make education more efficient (Chubb and Moe, 1990). As with other neoclassical policy proposals, this one too has not met the test of the real world very well. Places that have experimented with vouchers have not experienced improved educational outcomes (Gardner, 2000). A Post Keynesian perspective, which stresses the importance of some degree of monopoly power, should have a lot to add to this debate. Also needed is a Post Keynesian policy for improving educational outcomes that can compete with neoclassical policy of education vouchers.

What is true of an aging population, productivity growth, and improving education is likewise true of most contemporary policy issues such as crime, health care, poverty, and environmental issues. In most cases, a Post Keynesian voice is conspicuously missing. As a result, traditional economics has provided the primary voice in these policy debates, creating, we believe, weak policy analysis.

If Post Keynesian economics is to move forward in the twenty-first century it must begin to take its unique theoretical perspective and apply it to the key policy issues of the day. It is time for Post Keynesians to join the debate on public policy questions such as how to best provide education and health care, developing strategies for community development, raising the minimum wage versus increasing government wage subsidies, and the effects of structural and institutional factors on poverty.

In addition to a greater focus on public policy, Post Keynesians need to turn to basic empirical work such as gathering data and using that data to establish the groundwork for evaluating public policy and for testing economic theory. Some efforts have already been made along these lines, but for Post Keynesian economics to provide a more viable alternative to neoclassical orthodoxy much more work remains to be done. Post Keynesians should be able to play a positive role here because of the open system perspective they employ, which Dow ably describes in Chapter 2.

To take just a few examples, Post Keynesians need to look at the empirical links between aggregate demand and the supply side, particularly its impact on the labor force. The importance of relative incomes on aggregate spending needs further exploration, as does the relative incentive effects and income effects of higher minimum wages and other social welfare policies. More work also needs to be done on how the financial sector actually impacts the real sector of the economy as well as growth convergence and currency speculation in a global economy. As Thomas Kuhn (1962) has pointed out, it is this sort of empirical work that sustains a paradigm and helps keep it going once it reaches maturity.

Besides empirical work and public policy discussions, Post Keynesians must also explore more carefully the consequences of moving from a closed economy to a global economy.

The end of Bretton Woods led to the introduction of flexible exchange rates and efforts to deregulate international capital markets. The consequence of these policies became evident in the 1980s with the debt crisis that plagued Mexico and other Latin American countries and the Asian currency crisis in the 1990s. As long as current trade policies stay in place we can expect to see this type of instability recurring in different world regions in the decades ahead.

Post Keynesians need to recommend international public policies to help create global economic stability and full employment. As John Smithin points out in Chapter 10, this remains an important unresolved issue in Post Keynesian thought.

Post Keynesians also need to re-examine export-led growth policies as a means of expanding domestic employment. This policy has been advocated by many Post Keynesians for the last two decades, but such policies have not led to worldwide full employment or to international economic stability. Nor is it likely that they can ever do so because the exports of one country are the imports of another country. Export-led growth is thus impossible for all countries to achieve in a global economy; in a way, it is an attempt to export unemployment to one's trading partners.

These issues are particularly important in the early twenty-first century as many industrialized countries cut their budgets and employ tight monetary policies. Godley and Martin (1999) point out that with worldwide overcapacity and slow growth in Japan and Europe, the American economy has kept the world economy afloat in the 1990s. And it is the spending of borrowed money by households and firms that has sustained growth in the US. However, greater private indebtedness cannot continue forever. At some point the rate of private spending in the US will slow; unless there is some type of worldwide fiscal boost to replace this spending, there is a good chance for a severe worldwide recession.

These three areas for future research (policy analysis, empirical studies, and a focus on the global economy) all need to be guided by the main Post Keynesian principles. As we have pointed out and explained in this *Guide*, there are several key Post Keynesian ideas that need to drive this future research – the importance of fundamental uncertainty, the importance of institutions and historical time, the dominance of income effects over substitution effects, and a vision that unregulated, free markets do not necessarily lead to optimal outcomes. By taking such a tack, Post Keynesian economics can play a more influential role in the twenty-first century.

References

Chubb, J.E. and Moe, T.M. (1990) *Politics, Markets and America's Schools*, Washington, DC: Brookings Institution.

Eichner, A.S. (1978) *A Guide to Post Keynesian Economics*, Armonk, NY: M.E. Sharpe.

Gardner, H. (2000) "Paroxysms of Choice," *New York Review of Books*, 19 October: 44–9.

Godley, W. and Martin, B. (1999) "How Negative Can U.S. Saving Get?" *Policy Notes*, The Jerome Levy Economics Institute.

Gordon, D. (1995) "Putting the Horse (Back) Before the Cart: Disentangling the Macro Relationship between Investment and Savings," in G. Epstein and H. Gintis (eds.) *Macroeconomic Policy after the Conservative Era: Studies in Investment, Savings and Finance*, New York, Cambridge University Press, pp. 57–108.

Kuhn, T. (1962) *The Structure of Scientific Revolutions*, Chicago: University of Chicago Press.

Palley, T. (1996) "The Savings-Investment Nexus: How It Works and Why It Matters," Center for Economic Policy Analysis Working Paper.

Index